· Extraordinary · GOLF

THE ART OF THE POSSIBLE

Fred Shoemaker

with Pete Shoemaker

A Perigee Book

A PERIGEE BOOK
Published by the Penguin Group
Penguin Group (USA) Inc.
375 Hudson Street, New York, New York 10014, USA
Penguin Group (Canada), 90 Eglinton Avenue East, Suite 700, Toronto, Ontario M4P 2Y3, Canada
(a division of Pearson Penguin Canada Inc.)
Penguin Books Ltd., 80 Strand, London WC2R 0RL, England
Penguin Group Ireland, 25 St. Stephen's Green, Dublin 2, Ireland (a division of Penguin Books Ltd.)
Penguin Group (Australia), 250 Camberwell Road, Camberwell, Victoria 3124, Australia
(a division of Pearson Australia Group Pty. Ltd.)
Penguin Books India Pvt. Ltd., 11 Community Centre, Panchsheel Park, New Delhi—110 017, India
Penguin Group (NZ), 67 Apollo Drive, Rosedale, North Shore 0632, New Zealand
(a division of Pearson New Zealand Ltd.)
Penguin Books (South Africa) (Pty.) Ltd., 24 Sturdee Avenue, Rosebank, Johannesburg 2196,
South Africa

Penguin Books Ltd., Registered Offices: 80 Strand, London WC2R 0RL, England

While the author has made every effort to provide accurate telephone numbers and Internet addresses
at the time of publication, neither the publisher nor the author assumes any responsibility for errors,
or for changes that occur after publication. Further, the publisher does not have any control over and
does not assume any responsibility for author or third-party websites or their content.

PRINTING HISTORY
G. P. Putnam's Sons edition / May 1996
First Perigee edition / April 1997

Perigee trade paperback ISBN: 0-399-52276-X

The Library of Congress has catalogued the G. P. Putnam's Sons edition as follows:

Shoemaker, Fred.
Extraordinary golf: the art of the possible / by Fred Shoemaker
   with Pete Shoemaker.
      p.   cm.
      ISBN 0-399-14153-7
1. Golf—Study and teaching. 2. Golf—Psychological aspects.
I. Shoemaker, Pete. II. Title.
GV962.5.S56   1996   95-50975   CIP
796.352'07—dc20

PRINTED IN THE UNITED STATES OF AMERICA

30   29   28   27   26   25   24   23

Most Perigee Books are available at special quantity discounts for bulk purchases for sales promo-
tions, premiums, fund-raising, or educational use. Special books, or book excerpts, can also be created to fit specific needs. For details, write: Special Markets, Penguin Group (USA) Inc., 375 Hudson
Street, New York, New York 10014.

ACKNOWLEDGMENTS

I would like to thank the following people, who were instrumental in the creation of this book:

Tim Gallwey, whose Inner Game principles have helped guide me in teaching thousands of golf lessons.

My coaching partners John Allen, Garry Lester, Tom Nordland, Michael Lach, Kim Larsen, Steve McGee, Bill Condaxis, Evan Schiller, and Victor Whipp.

My own coach, Garry Lester, who has helped me become aware of what training and development is all about.

My friend and colleague Steve Cohen, and the members of the Shivas Irons Society.

The coaches at Landmark Education.

My family, who have supported me throughout, and particularly my brother and co-author Pete, who organized all the material and made a book of it.

My best friend and mate Johanne Hardy.

And Michael Murphy, whose *Golf in the Kingdom* touched me deeply, as it has so many other golfers.

CONTENTS

FOREWORD:
A GAME WORTH
PLAYING

Years ago I had a crisis in my golfing life.

I had grown up loving golf, and had played it at a very high level throughout my school years. But a few years after college, at a time when I had the opportunity and the backing to try for the pro tour, I soured on the game. The joy, the fascination—the magic—that had been so much a part of golf for me was almost gone, and I didn't know how to get it back. So I left the game completely.

I traveled halfway around the world, to a different continent and a different culture, but I still couldn't get away from golf. To paraphrase an old saying, "You can take the boy out of the golf course, but . . ." I realized that the game meant a lot to me, and I didn't want to give it up. What I needed was to play a different game from the one I had been playing.

I knew that I would probably be involved with golf for the rest of my life. I thought about all the time and energy I would be spending on the game, and I began to wonder what real value I could gain from it that would justify investing a significant portion of my life. I began to wonder what type of game would really be worth playing.

The game I *had* been playing was mostly concerned with the game I thought I *should* play: getting the respect of my peers, living up to the expectations of my friends and family, having the "right" swing. I knew what all that was about, and I didn't want it anymore. For the first time, I started to think about the type of game that I myself would like to play, the one that would give me the most joy and satisfaction, that would enrich my life the most.

I knew that it would not be bound by formulas, as my previous game had been. Looking back on my golf history, I saw that as the formulas came in, the joy went out. It became apparent to me that the element that was missing from my game—the ingredient that had made my early golfing years so magical—was freedom. I knew then that a game worth playing would be one in which I was free.

Now, the word *free* is used so often and in so many ways that it can be difficult to figure out exactly what it means. But my experience over the years has helped me. I have given more than 30,000 individual golf lessons, conducted hundreds of seminars for amateurs and professionals in several countries, led the Golf in the Kingdom workshop at the Esalen Institute for the past eight years, and run my own School for Extraordinary Golf for the past four. In this time I've learned some things about the meaning of freedom in golf.

It means that when you step up to a shot, if you think of formulas, checklists, or swing keys, you're not free. If you think that looking good and not being embarrassed are most important, you're not free. If your actions are shaped by fear, or even hope, you're not free. Freedom is stepping up to a shot as if you were the very first golfer, unburdened by past history, with a future full of possibilities. Freedom is thinking, "What shot would I hit if it were just up to me?" Which it is.

A person who can play this way is, in my opinion, the only person who is playing real golf. Everything else is golf with an asterisk, a footnote, a disclaimer. What about score? Although most people believe that getting the "right" swing and hitting the "right" shots will lead to the best scores, that has not been my experience. The freedom that I am describing is the basis for truly excellent, exceptional—extraordinary—golf. As in any other endeavor, whether work or play, the more freedom, enjoyment, and enthusiasm you experience, the better the performance. The freedom makes it all happen, and there is no freedom in formula.

I believe the real purpose of games is to teach us things that will be valuable for the rest of our lives. I also believe, as this book will show, that the way you do anything is the way you do everything. I hope that this book will help you see how you "are" on the golf course, and help you open yourself up to a freedom that you may rarely have experienced in your game, or your life. This freedom is what turns ordinary into extraordinary. Most people's lives have long periods of ordinary and short periods of extraordinary, and I would like to help reverse that trend.

So what is a game worth playing? Every person has to

decide that for him- or herself. The purpose of this book is to show you that the game of golf you are playing is not the only possible one. The purpose of this book is to show you that there are extraordinary possibilities that you may not yet have imagined.

HOW TO READ THIS BOOK

When people pick up a golf book for the first time, they generally leaf through it, often focusing on the diagrams and illustrations. Their point of view is shaped by the particular part of their game that they're currently most concerned about—driving, sand shots, putting—and they're usually looking for help in that specific area. They tend to read from that perspective, filtering the information in search of a few nuggets. You know how you go through a big pile of mail looking for a paycheck? Something like that.

No one can be taught anything unless he or she is ready and willing to learn. If you are looking for tips on particular problem areas of your game, this is not the book for you. You've probably figured that out by now. To get the most out of this book, you need to broaden your perspective. Instead of reading small, read big. Instead of looking for the solution to a particular problem, take a fresh look at how you approach the game of golf. Instead of judging what's right or wrong, open yourself up to what's possible. If you do, you will be already well on the road to extraordinary golf and the wonderful experiences that can result from playing the game in a new way.

EXTRAORDINARY GOLF

Chapter One

THE COURSE WALK

To begin, I'd like to invite you to take a walk with me around a golf course. Any course will do, so why don't you envision the one you're most familiar with. We're just going to walk a few holes, and you don't need to bring any clubs. I have a seven-iron and a few golf balls, and that's all we'll need. I take this walk with many of my students because it's an excellent way to introduce them to the main themes and ideas of *Extraordinary Golf*. I feel it's an ideal way to start the book.

So here we are on the first tee, and I'd like to tell you what this walk is all about.

If an average golfer takes 90 shots in a round, and each shot takes about two seconds, that adds up to only about three minutes of actual play. The pre-shot routine takes anywhere from five to ten seconds, which adds another ten minutes or so. That leaves more than three hours and forty-five minutes of time between shots in a typical four-hour round—about 95 percent of the round. This is time when you are simply out on the course, walking (or riding) to your next shot.

The traditional method of teaching golf focuses almost exclusively on the 5 percent of swing time and ignores the other 95 percent of the round. I've come to realize that the people who are most likely to improve beyond what is ordinary are people who have mastered the time between shots. I'm not talking about strategy or positive thinking or simply "doing things differently." I'm talking about a new way to "be" out on the course. I'm talking about being a golfer. The best and most lasting changes take place when a person is essentially "being different."

THE PACKAGE

Have you ever taken the time to notice what you bring with you to the first tee? I don't mean equipment, I mean the things you can't see—the things inside you. If you're like most golfers, you have some doubt, excitement, fear, key swing thoughts, desires, and a lot of hope. This is the package of the typical golfer, resulting from the way he or she has played and practiced the game. This package has three main points, and I'd like you to see if these fit you in any way.

First, most golfers come to the first tee committed only to looking good (hitting a good shot) and not being embarrassed. This desire for others' approval is so basic that most golfers are not even aware of it. It is the medium in which they live, much like water for a fish and air for a bird. The fact that this desire is so common as to be unnoticeable makes it even more entrenched in the golfer's mind, and it can easily overpower other commitments that a golfer might try to have.

Second, golfers are full of judgments about everyone and everything. This person has a better swing; I'm feeling so-so today; the weather will make things tougher, etc. Evaluations and judgments are being made all the time.

Third, no matter where they are on the golf course, most golfers are always just two shots away from being crazy. No matter how well they're playing, a couple of bad shots in a row can change their entire experience. They are always on the verge of being upset.

To recap:

1. uncommitted, except to looking good
2. constantly judging
3. always on the verge of being upset.

Now, with a package like this, it is very difficult to achieve and sustain extraordinary play. It's important to become aware of the package and then redesign it, and that is what this course walk is meant to help you do.

COMMITMENT

I mentioned that most golfers come to the first tee un-committed to anything except looking good and not being embarrassed. If this is your only commitment, I can guar-antee that your golfing experience will be erratic and often filled with anxiety—a very ordinary experience at best. It will be constantly subject to the vagaries of chance and na-ture, and can turn sour at any moment (two shots from being crazy). Consider replacing this hidden default com-mitment with a more desirable one of your own choosing.

The rules of golf say only that we should try to score as low as possible. They do not say what the purpose of the game is. That is for each person to determine. Why do *you* play this game? What would you really like to get out of it? It's likely that you spend a lot of your time and money on golf, so what would make it most worthwhile for you?

There is tremendous freedom in playing a game that you choose to play, rather than one you think you should play. Once you begin to uncover your own personal rea-sons for being out here, you can use them to form power-ful, inspiring commitments that will free you from the constant pressure of "looking good." There are any num-ber of possibilities: playing for enjoyment, to make new friends, to overcome fear, to learn to trust yourself—and you can certainly have different commitments at different times. The important thing is that they are freely chosen and that they have value to you. These new commitments are crucial in learning how to play golf in a new way.

EXTROSPECTION

The constant judgments that golfers make come from an ongoing inner dialogue. So when you're on the first tee, instead of being inside yourself and worrying, hoping, and judging like you usually do, why don't you try taking a look outside yourself? Instead of being introspective, be extrospective. Look around, see where you are and whom you're with. Actually meet your playing partners, instead of just shaking their hands and not really seeing them or remembering their names. One thing I've noticed consistently over the years is that enjoyment in golf always shows up when "you" disappear. When your thoughts aren't so much about you and your game, the experience is much more joyful.

Focus your attention on the real things before you: your body, the club, the ball, and the course. If you are going to play extraordinary golf, it will come from these things. I've noticed that most people can't pay attention to what's really happening because there is so much rattling around in their heads. Consider becoming extrospective.

I'm going to hit some shots here, and I'd like you to watch them. How high are they? When do they begin to descend? How far do they go? How do they curve? How many bounces do they take? Really look, really notice. Put your awareness *out there* instead of inside your head. By focusing your attention on real things and not on your internal dialogue, your mind will begin to calm down.

Now as we walk down the fairway, try to look at the

course in an artistic, rather than functional, way. If I were to set up a canvas and ask you to paint what you see, how would you do it? Notice the different colors, the shadows, the curve of the land. Even though you may have walked this course many, many times, have you ever really seen it? Look with the eyes of an artist, not a mechanic.

And as you walk, keep your eyes up and level with the horizon. Breathe easily and deeply and let your arms swing freely. Allow yourself freedom of movement. The typical golfer walks stiffly with head down, mulling over the last shot or the next shot, noticing very little. Now is the time to be different.

CREATIVITY

Here we are for our approach shots to the green. What would you hit from here? An eight-iron? How would you hit it—high, trying to drop it right in? When I ask these questions of my students, I find that players of similar ability almost always hit the same type of shot. Some need to check the yardage marker first, letting the club selection automatically follow. If someone unfamiliar with golf were to observe this process, I think he or she would conclude that most of us play an incredibly boring game. We're like one-trick ponies: 125 yards? Give me an eight-iron; 140? A seven-iron. Push a button, get a shot. Is it any wonder that most of us feel stuck in our same old game? Where's the variety, the creativity?

When I was very young and starting to learn the game, I would often go to the golf course with just one club. I found that I could make it do just about everything I needed—high, low, fade, hook. I learned everything about that club. My teaching experience now tells me that the best way to learn how to hit the ball straight is not to try to hit straight, as most people do on the practice range. The best way is to learn the full range of what one club can do. But when was the last time you saw someone on the range trying to hit hooks, fades, high lobs, and low runners? Everyone tries and tries to hit the ball straight, but few can do it consistently.

Most people think, "When I get my swing down, then I'll get to all that other stuff." But the truth is, you are never going to "get your swing down" *until* you get the other stuff. The other stuff comes first.

So let's see what other kind of shot we can hit from here. We could hit a draw shot, bringing the ball in from the right side to avoid the trap in front. Or we could run one right through the trap and use the sand to slow it down to hold the green. Or we could open up the face and really fly one in, using the extra height to stop it dead. The point is that we now have choices, and those choices allow us to approach our shots creatively, instead of mechanically.

My gut feeling is that in golf you're either creating or you're dying. I think that what makes great players stand out is that they approach all their shots with this same sense of creativity. They don't always have to hit the unusual shot, and more often than not their shots will be the expected ones. But they can hit their standard 140-yard eight-iron with the same feeling of creativity that you would use on a miracle recovery shot from in the trees— the one you have to hit through a foot-wide opening in the branches and bounce off the cart path, the one that makes your whole round and that you talk about for hours afterward. Imagine bringing that level of interest and excitement to all your shots!

AWAKENING

So now that we've hit some balls onto the green, let's see what they will do on their way to the hole. Students always ask me the secret to reading greens. I tell them that the secret is the same one that applies to all areas of golf: Stay awake! I find that very few golfers actually stay awake for an entire round. They seem to "check out" at many points along the way. Instead of noticing what's happening around them—being extrospective—they go back inside their heads and experience their same old stuff. As a result, instead of getting a new, unique experience every day, they get the same experience over and over. Is this characteristic of your game?

I have been fortunate to have had good coaches in my golf career. Tim Gallwey, author of *The Inner Game of Golf,* is one of them. Tim coached me on many things, among them how to stay awake. One time thereafter I took a trip to Ireland with my friend Steve Cohen and other members of the Shivas Irons Society. We played ten golf courses. When I returned, I realized that I could remember every hole we played, every shot that I took, and every shot that Steve took. And Steve didn't really want me to remember all his shots. Golf has become such a fascinating, passionate experience for me that I find I can't forget it. My goal as a teacher is to help my students experience the game in a similar way.

Back to the green. Watch this putt—all the way—and see what it actually does. Where does it break? How far does it break? How far in front of or behind the hole does it stop? Did you notice a tendency in yourself to watch only until you determined whether or not the putt did what you expected and not really pay attention to the rest? Although other techniques can enhance your skill, the basic key to reading greens is to be alert to and fascinated by what is happening at that moment—to be fully awake. Any child can do it, and I've met many people who have been playing more than forty years who haven't got a clue.

A REAL FUTURE

Let's move on to the second tee. Now I'd like to talk about something that all golfers know only too well: bad shots. Why do you get upset when you hit a bad shot? The answer may seem obvious, but I'd like you to think about it. Common reponses I get are: It didn't meet my expectations; it spoiled my score; it was embarrassing; I lost some money, and so on. But in my experience, none of these is the real reason that people get upset. I'd like you to consider another possibility. I believe that the real reason people get upset after a bad shot is that *they think they are going to do it again.*

Sound strange? Let me use an example to prove my point. Let's say you knew for a fact that you would top your first tee shot, but after that you were going to play the best round of your life. What would your reaction be after that first shot? I think the shot wouldn't bother you a bit, and you might even say, "Hooray, I got it out of the way!" The key to this change in attitude is that you know you have a bright future, a future that is not determined by your past.

Let me illustrate. I'll hold the golf club parallel to the ground, with one hand at each end. Let this club represent the past to the present moment, beginning at the club head, moving along the shaft, and ending at the end of the

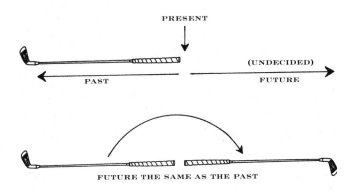

FUTURE THE SAME AS THE PAST

grip. The future extends out past the grip, and for the moment is undetermined—full of possibility. Most golfers simply take the past, lay it over into the future, and relive it again and again. I can demonstrate here by flipping this club over.

However, your future is *not* determined by your past. Just because you did something once does not mean that you will do it again. Yet most golfers play as if that were the case. You know those voices in your head: "There goes that slice again! I always slice. I don't know how to get rid of it. . . ." The key to extraordinary golf is keeping open your possibilities and your future. It *is* possible that you could hit an extraordinary shot. I'm not talking about simple positive thinking—I don't advocate that because it has not worked for me—nor am I saying you should set yourself up for disappointment by having unrealistic expectations. What I am saying is this: Have the courage to keep your possibilities open. Since most people play as if the future were decided, is it any wonder that most golfers play a boring, predictable game? Is it any wonder that they feel stuck and unable to make significant progress? A simple, courageous change in point of view completely transforms the golfing experience and the person who is playing.

Here, step up to the tee and take the seven-iron. Let's say your last two iron shots were badly sliced. How do you approach this one? Pretty defensively? Hoping for the best but really expecting to hit another clunker? Probably so. Do you think this attitude would be reflected in your body language, in the "air" about you as you set up? Do you think it might be noticeable to someone watching? The next time you watch a tournament, look at how golf professionals approach their shots. Then look at the players on your home course. In most cases you can tell an exceptional player from an average one before you even see them swing. Now let's try something different with your shot here. Let go of what you did before. Approach this shot with a new perspective—that it's possible that you could hit it sweet and true. Don't calculate the odds of this happening, just let it be a possibility, because it is undeniably possible. Don't you think this would make a difference in the way you approached the ball, a difference that would be visible to someone watching you?

In a fundamental sense, there would be a different person hitting the shot. This is what I mean about "being different" on the course, and the effect it can have. You aren't doing anything different, really—in both cases you are preparing to hit the ball. But the essential experience—and the result—could be dramatically different. Keeping possibilities open is the key.

I have found that extraordinary people are able to keep these possibilities open all the time. They play a game that is full of promise and excitement. They are a delight to play with, and their learning, performance, and enjoyment of the game go far beyond that of most people. This point of view is the cornerstone of extraordinary golf. The time between shots is a time to put the past in the past, create a future that is powerful and full of possibility, and live into that future.

SUMMARY

The "package" that most golfers bring with them to the course consists of the following: (1) being committed only to looking good; (2) being judgmental; and (3) being on the verge of feeling upset. However, it's possible to redesign this package. Instead of living out hidden, undesirable commitments, determine your own valuable reasons for playing the game and make commitments based on those reasons. Instead of being judgmental and introspective, become extrospective and focus your attention on the real things out there: the club, the ball, your body, and the golf course. See the course through fresh, artistic eyes, and be awake to what is happening at all times. Instead of always playing on the edge of being upset, realize that your future is not determined by your past, and use the time between shots to create a future that is full of exciting possibilities.

The time between shots—95 percent of a round of golf—is when this new, redesigned package takes shape. The result is a new way of "being" on the course; in a sense, there is a new person playing the game. What follows is a new and extraordinary game of golf.

This course walk is meant to be an introduction to the basic ideas of the book, and the points I've made here will be discussed in greater detail. But now it's time for breakfast. As we walk back—eyes up, breathing deeply, arms swinging freely—let's take the time to appreciate being here. It's a beautiful day, and we're taking a walk in a beautiful garden. That's what golf really is, and there's no reason that this wonderful feeling should change just because we happen to have a bag of clubs with us.

Enjoy. See you back at the clubhouse.

INTERLUDE: MY STORY

I'd like to give you a little background on myself and a story about a round of golf that changed my life.

I started learning how to play golf when I was nine years old on the island of Guam. My father was a Naval officer and our family was stationed there. Dad was an avid golfer and a good coach, in that he really didn't coach me too much, but let me experiment and find my own ways of doing things. I took to the game right away, and by age twelve was a real prodigy. I had an ideal setup: a convenient course, time to learn and experiment, and the support of my friends and family without any pressure or competition. I wish all kids could learn the game under similar conditions. I grew to love golf and everything about it: the playing, the practicing, the atmosphere, the camaraderie—it was a wonderful time.

When we moved back to the States, I played on my high school golf team and for the first time experienced competition and pressure. Even though I won quite often—I was the top player on the team—golf became less and less fun. This pattern continued through college, and by the time I graduated I had really lost my enthusiasm for the game. Although I was playing pretty well, I felt I was stuck and not making any real improvement. And I seemed to be surrounded by people who felt the same way.

Everywhere I looked I saw golfers who never seemed to play up to their full potential and were always complaining about some aspect of their game. They never seemed to "get" golf—to become the golfers they wanted to be. I felt I was becoming just like them. Even though friends offered to back me if I wanted to try for the pro tour, I had no real desire to take them up on it. The whole experience of golf came to look very narrow to me, consisting only of practicing, playing, and talking about golf. It seemed very unsatisfying, and I found myself wondering why anyone would want to do this for a living.

When I looked for someone to discuss my dissatisfaction with, to try to help me sort out what I was feeling, I found no help. Anyone would go on at length with me about my backswing or my grip, but no one, not even the coach, seemed to have a clue how to approach other aspects of the game. On the surface, I looked like a pretty successful golfer, but underneath I was not a happy camper.

However, I had just graduated from college and I needed a job, so when the golf coach position at the college opened up, I took it. I was comfortable being around all my friends and I hoped I might be able to bring out other aspects of the game that I thought were important. I did my best, but I just wasn't ready for coaching, and I became discouraged. Like many people experience in their first job after school, my ideals took a beating.

One instance that stands out in my mind happened right before I was about to take the team to the main tournament of the year. I was talking with the athletic director and he asked me what I wanted for the team. I answered that I wanted the guys to play well with good sportsmanship, enjoy themselves, and have an experience they could remember fondly for the rest of their lives. The athletic director chuckled and said I sounded like a recreational supervisor. This was intercollegiate sports, he said, and the important thing was to place as high as possible, hopefully to win. I had assumed that all the things I had mentioned would lead to the team playing their best, but they seemed irrelevant to the athletic director. I felt foolish and began to have doubts about the importance of the things that had most concerned me. So after two years of coaching, I decided to do something different with my life.

INTO AFRICA

I joined the Peace Corps and was assigned to teach high school in Africa. The new challenges and the new friends did me a world of good, as did the opportunity to help others and not worry so much about my own problems.

After the usual training and travel adventures, I found my-self teaching in a small village in central Ghana.

Needless to say, golf is not big in equatorial Africa, and that was just fine with me. But after a few months of teaching, I got homesick for the game. I knew there was at least one golf course in the country, because on the way to the village I had seen it, just outside the capital city, Accra. It wasn't quite what I was used to—the fairways were indistinguishable and the greens were really "browns"—but I was in no position to be picky. I wanted to tee it up.

So I wrote a letter to the course saying that I was an American golf professional—I thought that would help—and asking if I could play a round sometime during my upcoming Christmas break. I received a quick and enthusiastic reply. I was on! They would be expecting me on the morning of December 28 (I remember that date because it was two days before a military coup took place, but that's another story). The next thing to do was to get some clubs.

When I got to Accra I called the U.S. embassy—and I was in luck. It turned out that a previous U.S. ambassador had left behind a set of clubs that I was welcome to. And that previous U.S. ambassador to Ghana just happened to have been Shirley Temple Black. So there I was, about to play golf in Africa with Shirley Temple's golf clubs. About this time I began to realize that no matter what else came out of this, it was going to be a good golf story.

When I arrived at the course on the morning of the twenty-eighth, a fairly large crowd had gathered on the first tee. I was met by the people in charge and introduced to the crowd as the American golf champion. I was then introduced to a handsome, alert, cheerful man about my age and height who was going to be my playing partner. He had what seemed to be the standard attire for the course—T-shirt, shorts and bare feet—and carried a set of clubs that would have been at home in the Smithsonian Institution. His name was Kojo, and he was the Ghanaian golf champ. We were going to play a match.

My first reaction, after surprise, was right in line with my Peace Corps training—Be a good ambassador. Don't beat him too badly, make it a close, exciting game, and everyone will be happy. Another thought also popped into my head, along the lines of "I've always wanted to be the best golfer in the country, maybe I've finally found the right country!" I was looking forward to an enjoyable round.

Considering the conditions and the layoff that I'd had, I started out playing pretty well. So did Kojo, however, and even though I was playing full out, I was only one up after nine holes. Kojo was certainly talented, but not exceptionally so, and he obviously had had limited instruction and experience. But he seemed to get the most out of his ability and was really enjoying the game.

As we began the back nine my attitude started to change. I just wanted to win. I didn't even want to think about the embarrassment of losing the match. My game, of course, changed as well, and not for the better. Kojo seemed to play the same as before. He pulled even at 11 and at 16 he went one up. On 17 he sank a ten-footer for the match. The last I saw of him he was being carried toward the clubhouse on the shoulders of the crowd.

A GOLF LESSON

I put on a game face, of course. I laughed and made "good ambassador" jokes, but on the inside I felt humiliated. Even knowing that if we played ten matches I would win most of them didn't take the sting out of this one loss. But this was a time in my life when, thankfully, I was able to learn from adversity. Over the next few days I began to understand what had happened out there on the course.

Even though Kojo and I were both playing golf, we were playing vastly different games. My game, especially on the back nine, was concerned with performance and avoiding embarrassment—looking good. His game—well, I'm not really sure what he was experiencing, but he seemed to be playing with a joy and a sense of freedom that I had rarely seen. My game filled me with anxiety and self-doubt and made me play worse than I was able to play. His game allowed him to play far closer to his potential.

It began to dawn on me that in order to play the type of golf that I'd always aspired to, I had to play a different game than the one I'd been playing all these years. I also began to understand that in order to play this different game, I had, in essence, to become a different person. The "me" who played the game had to change. At the time, I didn't have a clue how to do that, but I was sure I wanted to try.

That round with Kojo was one of only three I played in my two years in Ghana, so I had plenty of time to think about it. Being in a different, faraway culture gave me a unique perspective on my whole past golfing experience. As when a landscape is viewed from a distance, the important things began to stand out. What came through to me loud and clear was that I really did love the game and that it could have plenty of meaning in my life and other people's lives. There was a lot more to golf than most people realized. I really began to miss it, way back there in the jungle, and I wanted to play again.

SPECIAL DELIVERY

It can be difficult to get mail when you're in the Peace Corps, especially if you're 150 miles from the coast in an African jungle. The only way we could get large items from home was through diplomatic pouches, which were picked up in Accra and delivered periodically by a Corps person acting as a courier—an arduous trip. I wrote my parents and asked them to pouch me a few golf clubs, and to label them "teaching materials"—the only way they would get through. Little did I know how true that white lie would turn out to be.

A teacher from my school was acting as the courier, and he picked up my large package, not knowing what it was. Transportation consisted of large flatbed trucks called *trow-trows,* which had overhead rails like subway cars. People would stand tightly packed in the back of the trucks and grab the overhead bars for support. My fellow teacher carried my clubs and other mail and packages for hours in a truck like this, banging over rough jungle roads. When he arrived at my house with the package, I was so embarrassed by the fact that it was golf clubs that I wouldn't open it. Of course he was dying to see what he had lugged all that way. There he was, beaming like an expectant father, and I wouldn't show him the baby!

Later on, in the privacy of my room, I took them out. They were just some old clubs, but boy, they looked great. I took a few swings and all the good feelings came back. The next day I took the few golf balls that my folks had included in the pouch, hid a nine-iron down my pants leg, and went out to hit a few. There were no grassy fields in the jungle, and the only open place was a soccer field that had been cleared down to the ground by machete. But it was Pebble Beach to me as I became totally involved in hitting balls back and forth.

After a while I looked up and realized that several kids had gathered to watch me, fascinated by something they'd never seen before. One of them came up and said politely,

"Sir, what are you doing?" Somewhat embarrassed, I answered that I was playing golf. "Why are you doing this?" he said. "What is it for?" It's hard to imagine a situation where hitting a golf ball could look more ludicrous and irrelevant, but as I stood there suddenly I knew that there was a great reason for playing this game. It wasn't any particular word that came to my head, it was a feeling, a glimpse of the wonderful possibilities that this game had. I stopped playing and never hit balls there again, but it was enough. That was my first small step on the road that I'm still on. I wasn't aimless anymore.

Chapter Two

PURPOSE

$\mathbf{A}$t almost every workshop that I've given, the first thing I do after introductions is ask the students two questions. First, "Why do you play golf?" Second, "What would you like to get out of this workshop?" I've taught in several different countries, yet the answers I get are always similar. I write the responses on a flip chart. Here is what a typical one looks like:

WHY DO YOU PLAY?	WHAT DO YOU WANT FROM THE WORKSHOP?
The challenge	Stop my slice
To be with friends	Improve my score
Like to walk in nature	Correct my form
Good vacation activity	Achieve more power
Like to learn new things	Learn the short game
Joy of accomplishment	Get out of bunkers
Game my spouse and I can play together	Learn course management
Develop confidence	Hit more solid shots
Like competition	Learn how to make short putts
Can play all my life	Improve alignment
Develop concentration	

I'd like you to take a look at this chart for a minute and see if it seems like something you might write down for yourself. Are the things on the left reasons why golf appeals to you, and are the things on the right what you look for when you take a lesson or attend a workshop? Are you beginning to see what I'm up to here? Do you realize that these are trick questions? Very few people do.

Most golfers believe that if they get the things on the right, it will lead to getting those on the left. In fact, many think that if they do not get the things on the right, they will never be able to get those on the left. This approach can be summed up by the statement: "If I play better, then I'll enjoy the game more." This point of view is so universal that almost no one questions it, but my experience tells me that it is completely false.

After twenty years of teaching golf, I have learned that if you lower your handicap, get the correct form, get out of bunkers in one shot rather than two, etc., it will have no effect on your overall happiness and fulfillment from the game. I wouldn't have said that ten years ago. I used to think that if people got better, they'd be happier. However, having watched people over the years improve by leaps and bounds—watched them get the stuff on the right side of the chart—I've realized that the stuff on the left does not automatically follow.

These are trick questions because they really ask the same question, and I believe they should elicit the same answers. Doesn't it make sense that if you play golf to develop confidence or concentration, you would go to a workshop seeking to learn about confidence and concentration? That if you like to learn new things, you would want to find out more about how you learn? Almost no one approaches golf in this way.

There is nothing wrong with the things on the right, but they don't last very long. If you learn to hit the ball farther than you used to, you'll still want to hit it even a little farther. If you lower your score, you'll always feel that you could lower it just a little more. If I were to sum up the things on the left side of the chart—why people play golf—I would do it in four words: joy, satisfaction, personal growth, and fulfillment. Most people try for the things on the right and hope that someday they will feel the joy, satisfaction, growth, and fulfillment that they really want. But unfortunately, for most people that someday never comes.

THE ETERNAL TRIANGLE

As Tim Gallwey wrote in *The Inner Game of Golf,* there are three main parts to everyone's golfing experience, which can be shown best as an equilateral triangle:

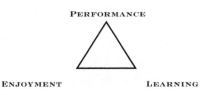

PERFORMANCE

ENJOYMENT   LEARNING

If you look at the list from the workshop, you'll notice that the entire right side is about performance, while the left is about learning and enjoyment. While people cite learning and enjoyment as primary reasons for playing golf, they focus almost entirely on performance when they actually play. However, things work best when all three parts are kept in balance. The paradox is that too much focus on performance throws things out of balance and lessens your ability to perform well. To recap, if you focus solely on the things on the right side of the chart, it will be very difficult to get those on the left. But if you focus on those on the left, the right side will take care of itself. Learning and enjoyment are the foundation for good performance—they always come first.

As I said in the course walk, extraordinary golf comes not from just doing things differently, but from a new way of being. The right side of the chart is about doing; the left side is about being. The ordinary way of proceeding is from right to left. Extraordinary golf results from the opposite approach—left to right. In other words, being precedes doing. Here's a story that will help illustrate what I mean.

A REAL REASON TO PLAY

Years ago I was playing in the California State Amateur tournament at Cypress Point in Monterey. Warming up on the putting green, I had the usual anxieties, but this time I changed my regular pre-tournament routine. I had been working recently with Tim Gallwey, and I did something that he coached me to do: I asked myself three questions.

The first question was "What's the worst that could happen?" I thought for a minute, and I figured that the worst would be to shoot about 85 and have to go back home and face the people there. I would be embarrassed. People would probably say things like "Fred's not a very good tournament player," "Did you hear he choked?" or, "He's been playing around with that mental stuff and look where it got him." People would listen to me less when I talked about golf, and I would go around wondering what they were thinking. It seemed like it would be pretty bad.

And then I wondered, "How long would that last?" Suddenly I realized that even in the worst scenario, no one would really care after about a week or two. It shocked me. The thing that I feared the most, that I had spent so much of my time working to avoid, would go away after a very short time. I might hold onto it for longer, but it wouldn't matter to anyone else. And this had ruled my practice and play for years! I took a look at the worst, and hey—it wasn't so bad.

The second question I asked was "What's the best that could happen?" Well, I'd shoot 66, prance around after the round, and get a lot of attention and some quotes in the paper. Everybody would say I was a great tournament player and pat me on the back. People would really admire me. And as I thought about this scenario, guess what? Another shock! After a short time, nobody would care about this either! And this is what I had longed for and dreamed about for years.

The best wasn't so good, and the worst wasn't so bad. My whole golfing life had been centered around achieving one and avoiding the other, and neither one amounted to a hill of beans. You know the expression "It hit me"? Well, it hit me.

The last question I asked myself, after considering both the best and the worst, was "What do I really want?" What do *I* want that's worth my time spent out there? What is something that will last a long time, that will give me dignity and integrity? When I walk off this golf course, what would I like to have achieved that will have been worth my time, energy, and money?

I sat down for a minute and thought about that. And for the first time in my life I realized that what I really wanted was to play a round of golf without fear. Just once, I wanted to be able to tee it up and not worry about the consequences, what people would say, what the papers would say. I just wanted to play and let it go—every time. I saw the worst, and it wasn't so bad. I saw the best, and it wasn't so good. I could choose what I really wanted for *me* this time, just for me.

So I teed it up and just let it go. I could accept whatever happened to my golf ball as long as fear wasn't involved. I was committed to playing without fear. I shot a 69 and led the tournament after the first round.

KEEP ON PUSHIN'

The desire for approval and the fear of embarrassment are just flip sides of the same record. And unfortunately, for most people it's a long-playing record. We say we hunger for achievement, but what we don't usually say is that we are terrified of lack of achievement. The best way to overcome this fear is to clarify it.

If we hear a noise in the dark we are easily frightened, not knowing what it is. Once we turn on the light and see that it is a tree branch or the cat our fear vanishes. Bringing our golf anxieties to light has the same effect; it can free us from them. A process such as asking the three questions above is the most effective way I have found to get to the heart of what we are afraid of. The important thing is to be persistent and keep probing, keep asking, "What am I *really* worried about?" I think you'll find, as I did, that fears in golf are like clouds: They seem solid and forbidding from a distance, but when you get close they are nothing but mist. And when you break through them, the sun really shines.

If "looking good" rules your golf experience, you're in for a very ordinary time. The performance aspect should not dominate your game, but that doesn't mean that you should ignore or devalue it—it has its rightful place in the overall triangle. We all want to play well. We all want to win, at least some of the time. And we all would like others to approve rather than disapprove of us. The problem is that we confuse the *goal* of the game, which is scoring as low as possible (winning), with the *purpose* of the game, which we decide for ourselves. This obsession with performance and winning dominates all games in our society, not just golf.

We all know the status of winning in the games of our culture. Yet if games were only about winning, as our society seems to shout, then lopsided victories—blowouts—should be the most enjoyable, since they represent winning in a big way. But of course this isn't the case, and the contests that are most memorable are the well-played, dramatic ones that seem to elevate both sides to a higher level, regardless of who wins. What we are really looking for in games is far deeper and richer than just winning.

I have no idea what the original intent was of the Scottish shepherds who presumably invented golf. Probably to while away some pretty boring hours in the fields. But it doesn't really matter, since we have the freedom to play the game for whatever reasons we choose. The goal of golf is to try to score as low as possible; that's what makes the game happen and makes the benefits possible. This goal is a vital part of the game and will be treated as such in this book. The purpose of golf is . . . for you to decide. As I asked earlier, Why do *you* want to play this game? What would you like to get out of it that would be worth all the time and money you spend on it? Throughout this book I'll be discussing a variety of interesting, inspiring reasons for playing this game and any game. I'm sure you have some that come to mind. In the meantime, I'd like to show you another way to approach this fundamental question, a way that has been very effective for me and my students.

SELF-ADDRESSED

Take a trip into the future and imagine that you are much older and near the end of your life. By some miracle you have the opportunity to write a letter to your current, younger self. This letter would be about golf and the way you've played the game all your life. Based on my experience with golfers, this is what I think that letter might say:

Dear Younger Me,

I can't play golf anymore. I tried to swing the club the other day but my body wouldn't cooperate. The best I can do now is sometimes take walks on the course, but my eyes aren't as good as they used to be so I don't see much. I have a lot of time to sit and think now, and I often think about the game.

It was my favorite game. I played most of my adult life. Thousands of rounds, thousands of hours practicing. As I look back, I guess I had a pretty good time at it. But now that I can't do it anymore, I wish I'd done it differently.

It's funny, but with all the time I spent playing golf, I never thought that I was a real golfer. I never felt that I was good enough to really belong out there. It doesn't make much sense, since I scored better than average and a lot of people envied my game, but I always felt that if I was just a little better or a little more consistent, then I'd really feel good. I'd be satisfied with my game. But I never was. It was always "one of these days I'll get it" or "one day I'll get there" and now here I am. I can't play anymore, and I never got there.

I met a whole lot of different people out on the course. That was one of the best things about the game. But aside from my regular partners and a few others, I don't feel like I got to know many of those people very well. I know they didn't really get to know me. At times they probably didn't want to. I was pretty occupied with my own game most of the time and didn't have much time for anyone else, especially if I wasn't playing well.

So why am I writing you this letter anyway, just to complain? Not really. Like I said, my golfing experience wasn't that bad. But it could have been so much better, and I see that so clearly now. I want to tell you, so you can learn from it. I don't want you getting to my age and feeling the same regrets I'm feeling now.

I wish, I wish. Sad words, I suppose, but necessary. I wish I could have played the game with more joy, more freedom. I was always so concerned with "doing it right" that I never seemed to be able to just enjoy doing it at all. I was so hard on myself, never satisfied, always expecting more. Who was I trying to please? Certainly not myself, because I never did. If there were people whose opinions were important enough to justify all that self-criticism, I never met them.

I wish I could have been a better playing partner. I wasn't a bad person to be with, really, but I wish I had been friendlier and gotten to know people better. I wish I could have laughed and joked more, and given people more encouragement. I probably would have gotten more from them, and I would have loved that. There were a few bad apples over the years, but most of the people I played with were friendly, polite, and sincere. They really just wanted to make friends and have a good time. I wish I could have made more friends and had a better time.

I'm inside a lot now, and I miss the beauty of the outdoors. For years when I was golfing I walked through some of the most beautiful places on earth, and yet I don't feel as if I really saw them. Beautiful landscapes, trees, flowers, animals, the sky, the ocean—how could I have missed so much? What else was I thinking of that was so important—my grip, my backswing, my stance? Sure, I needed to think about those sometimes, but so often as to be oblivious to so much beauty? And all the green—the wonderful, deep, lush color of green! My eyes are starting to fail. I wish I had used them better so I would have more vivid memories now.

So what is it that I'm trying to say? I played the type of game that I thought I should play, to please the type of people that I thought I should please. But it didn't work. My game was mine to play, but I gave it away. It's a wonderful game. Please, don't lose yours. Play a game that you want to play. Play a game that gives you joy and satisfaction and makes you a better person to your family and friends. Play with enthusiasm, play with freedom. Appreciate the beauty of nature and the people around you. Realize how lucky you are to be able to do it. All too soon your time will be up, and you won't be able to play anymore. Play a game that enriches your life.

That's all I have to say. I don't really know just how this letter will get to you, but I hope that it reaches you in time. Take care.

Love,
Older Me

Chapter Three

THE CULTURE OF GOLFERS

AWARENESS AND LEARNING

I've traveled extensively in my life, as a child with my Navy family, then as a Peace Corps volunteer, and finally as a golf teacher giving workshops. I have visited and taught in different countries and different cultures. Experiencing other cultures firsthand has made me aware of how much a culture can shape what a person does and how that person views the world. Every person's culture is, essentially, a deep, ingrained point of view.

Communication between cultures is often difficult because it can be hard to see things from a point of view other than your own. We all have heard about the types of problems that American businesspeople have in Japan, and vice versa. Training is necessary to bridge the gap. The first step in this training consists of seeing the limitations of your own cultural point of view and realizing that what you take for granted may not be the only way of looking at things. This awareness can help free you from the powerful pull of your own culture and help make another point of view possible. Cultures are like magnets that draw us into a particular way of acting and thinking. Until we can see the limitations of our own culture, we will often act in ways that are both predictable and intolerant.

Having taught golf in different cultures, I have noticed a point of view that transcends normal cultural boundaries and is common to all who play the game. In addition to all the obvious things we golfers have in common, there is one that is not so apparent. But it may be the most powerful. I call this the Culture of Golfers.

There is one basic principle in the Culture of Golfers, and it is this: *There is something wrong with my game, and I must fix it.* This is the point of view from which virtually all golfers see their game. It is so pervasive and taken for granted that almost no one notices it and almost no one can envision another way to approach the game. It is the way golfers view their practice and their instruction. Isn't it the reason you got this book—"Something is wrong with my game and maybe this book will help me fix it"? It seems impossible to imagine another effective way to look at golf, doesn't it, because if you don't try to fix what's wrong, how can you hope to improve? In the Culture of Golfers, this is the only way.

In this section of the book I will present you with another possible point of view—another culture. As in other cross-cultural training, the first step is awareness of the current culture and of how it affects everything you do, followed by the basic principles of the new culture. And like other cross-cultural experiences, it will take time to assimilate. You may understand the logic of it as you read it, but experiencing it on the golf course will take time and patience. Yet it will be well worth it. As sure as I am that the sun will rise tomorrow, I guarantee that if you can understand and experience this one principle, it will open up tremendous possibilities for improvement in your game.

THE GOLFER'S CONDITION

The phrase *the human condition* has a fatalistic, tragic overtone for most people in our culture. In this view of life, the odds against us are such that only true heroes can overcome them, and then only for a short time. The Culture of Golfers has a similar story: The golf swing is (pardon the expression) an unnatural act. Therefore all golfers must struggle mightily to achieve it. Constant vigilance is necessary because any slacking off will result in regression to our natural, ungolflike tendencies. Golf is difficult, and only a few—the heroes among us—are able to play it well enough to become real golfers. The rest of us are destined to hack away in the wilderness.

A little melodramatic? Perhaps, but you know as well as I do how seriously many golfers take their game. I feel that this is an accurate representation of the attitude most golfers have toward golf. Certainly no one has thought of it in these exact words—they probably never *thought* of it at all. The point is that everyone takes this view for granted, and that is why it is so powerful and so difficult to see. Check yourself. When you go to the range, what is your main thought? Probably it is "I need to work on something"—your swing has some flaws and you need to fix them. If you really want to improve, and all golfers do, how else can you do it?

I know this culture well. I lived in it for many years. I read the books, I took the lessons, I walked the walk, I talked the talk. I rode the roller coaster of "now I've got it, now I've lost it, now I've got it, now I've lost it." I felt the exhilaration when I "had it," I felt the frustration when I "lost it" and had no idea why. I've seen improvement, and I've seen that improvement level off until I was stuck in my same old game. I've been there, done that. I was a card-carrying member of the Culture of Golfers, and I can testify that it is, in a word, ordinary. There is another way.

FIX-ATION

I have sat next to more than 3,500 people while they watched videotapes of their golf swing, most of them seeing their swing for the first time. In addition to observing their videos with them, I have had the chance to observe them as they watched the tapes. In every film review session with every nonprofessional player, there has been one thing in common. Without exception, each person has been surprised by things that he or she has seen in the swing. The general reaction is "I had no idea I was doing that!" Every person has been completely unaware of large areas of their golf swing, utterly in the dark about what he or she was doing.

The basic principle of the old golf culture is: "There is something wrong with my swing, and I must fix it." Now I would like to ask a simple question: "Fix what?" Here's an imaginary conversation that captures the essence of my initial interactions with students:

"Fix what?"
"My golf swing."
"What part of your swing?"
"What I was doing wrong."
"What were you doing wrong?"
"I don't know."
"How will you know when it's fixed?"
"I'll hit the ball right."
"What if the ball goes wrong again?"
"I'll have to fix it."
"Fix what?"
"My golf swing."
Etc.

Sounds a bit like Abbot and Costello's "Who's on First?" routine, doesn't it? But the point is clear: How can you fix something when you don't know what it is? How can you correct what you're doing when you don't have any idea what you're doing? This may sound like a joke, but it is no joke. This is actually the way most golfers try to improve! Of course the results are unsatisfying.

Being constantly in "fix-it" mode is the legacy of the old Culture of Golfers. In that culture, there is no other way to practice. At the risk of repeating myself, *You cannot fix your golf swing unless you know what your golf swing is.* Awareness is the only thing that allows for development. Anything else is a shot in the dark. It's a roller coaster of "now I've got it, now I don't." It's tips that work and suddenly fail. It's playing "my best round ever," then two shots later—crazy. It's inconsistency and frustration. Sound familiar?

CULTURE SHOCK

So get ready for a little culture shock. The old culture says, "There is something wrong with my golf swing, and I must fix it." The new culture says this: "There is something going on in my golf swing, and I must be aware of it." And the best way to become aware of what you are doing is *not* to fix it. That's right, just leave it alone for a while, stop changing it, and simply take a look at what's there.

Imagine going to the range, practicing for an hour, and not once trying to "work on something." Imagine a whole practice session where you simply swing your regular way and just try to feel what it is that you are doing. Imagine a practice where, for once, you don't judge yourself on the quality of your shots but on the quality of your awareness and feel. Imagine not fixing it.

Now, in the old culture this idea is absurd and pointless. Since our swing is flawed to begin with, how can we hope to improve if we don't fix it? Let me show you why this principle of starting with awareness makes sense in the new culture. It has to do with a phenomenon that I have observed for years but only recently have begun to understand, that simple awareness leads to consistency and improvement.

I have seen it time and time again, with golfers of all skill levels. When people become more aware of key areas of their swing, their shots become more consistent. And this consistency is the beginning of great improvement. It's almost like magic. For the longest time I couldn't explain it, but I realize now that increased awareness allows the body's natural instincts to come into play, and these instincts make the swing more powerful and efficient. Awareness thus leads to improvement.

It's really the most natural thing in the world, when you think about it. It's how all real learning takes place. How does a child learn to walk? Certainly not by heeding verbal instructions from the parents—children don't even understand much language at that age. A child learns by trial and error, by awareness of action and result. "If I put my foot here, this happens. If I put my foot there, that happens." The child doesn't cloud his or her awareness by judging the results, the child simply observes the results, and very soon develops a feel for walking that lasts throughout life.

Increased awareness during the golf swing allows this

natural learning process to flourish. It is no mystery why a golf ball travels as it does—the laws of physics always hold true. If the club head strikes the ball in a certain way, the ball will travel accordingly every time. The awareness that begins with "not fixing it" allows learning to proceed like it does in a child. "If my hands do this, the ball goes this way. If my hands do that, the ball goes that way." You are soon able to feel what your hands do when the ball goes where you want, and this feel gives you a much greater chance of repeating desirable shots. It also takes much of the mystery out of why shots don't go where you want, which does a lot for your sanity.

Can you see how this natural learning cycle has been short-circuited in the old culture, making the results so unsatisfying? With a basic philosophy of "something's always wrong with what I'm doing," you depend on outside help to improve. By not developing an awareness of what you're actually doing—why bother since it will be wrong anyway—you omit an essential step in the natural learning process. The action-awareness-response feedback loop by which all essential actions are learned is disrupted, with results that we all know too well.

FROM BLINDNESS TO SIGHT

The old culture is based on judging what is right and wrong, paying little attention to what you are actually doing (since it is wrong), and looking outside yourself for the "right" way. Consider another approach based on becoming aware of what you are doing without judging it— simply developing a feel for what actions produce what results and letting the body's natural learning processes assist you. In the old culture you have no idea what's happening in your swing. In the new culture you become aware of what you are doing. In the old culture you are blind. In the new culture you begin to see. It's really that simple.

Does this feeling of blindness, and the anxiety and frustration associated with it, fit with your current experience of the game? It certainly does with the experiences I used to have. Take this one, for instance, which occurred during my college days:

I had been playing consistently pretty well for a number of rounds and had told my friends about my good scores. They were looking forward to playing with me, and of course I wanted to show them my improved game. I started the round hoping for the best, but at the third hole I started to lose it. I had no idea why. It seemed I was swinging the same way and I was using the same key swing thoughts, but the ball wasn't going where I wanted. I got angry, I started to press, and things went from bad to worse. My friends tried to be polite, but they had that look that said, "What was this guy saying about being improved?" I was frustrated, embarrassed, and miserable. The worst part was the fact that I had no idea what I was doing wrong and felt powerless to stop it. It was awful, and even though it happened many years ago, the memories are still vivid. Has anything like this ever happened to you?

The experience of being blind makes us feel helpless and vulnerable. It can make us approach the game with great anxiety since, as I described, there is always the possibility that things could suddenly fall apart in a very unpleasant way. It leads to inconsistent play as we continually grasp in the dark for solutions. As an old saying goes: "In the land of the blind, the one-eye is king." No wonder golfers are so willing to try out every new method and training gadget, no matter how ludicrous! When you have no idea what's going on, you try anything.

Let there be light.

LEARNING POSSIBILITIES

So how can you practice and play with a point of view other than "something is wrong"? What are your alternatives? Well, try this. Let's say you go to the driving range and start warming up. Your first instinct always is going to be "I want to work on something." You need to catch yourself right there, in that moment: "There it is! There's the Culture of Golfers—I want to fix it!" Be aware of the ingrained habits, the powerful pull of the old culture beginning to kick in. This awareness is the first step in being free of all that. Now, what else is there? Instead of seeing what's wrong, look for what's possible.

In the thousands of lessons I have given over the years I have noticed that the people who learn quickly and who play exceptional golf have something in common. Like all extraordinary and creative people, they look and feel for what's possible, instead of working from the point of view of "something's wrong." Unlike others, they don't waste a lot of time and energy in judging everything. They do not look for what is right or wrong, but simply for new possibilities. And they find them.

So as you practice, try to develop an awareness of your golf swing without judging it. In the latter part of this book I will describe specific exercises to help develop this awareness, including ways to coach others and have others coach you in this regard. Being nonjudgmental is essential because if you look through a filter of right/wrong, you will never see your swing clearly. It is important here to remember what I said earlier, that you may now understand this logically, but experiencing it will take time and patience, since the old conditioning runs deep. I urge you to stay with the awareness—I guarantee it will be worth it.

As you develop awareness and free yourself from the tyranny of right/wrong, try to loosen up and play around a little. Take a look at what's possible. Do things differently. Try different swings, different shots. Don't worry about the "right" way—you'll get to that. Try swinging in exaggerated ways—very far inside-out or outside-in, very slow. Try hitting all kinds of shots—high, low, hook, slice. All the while note what you do to produce those shots: hands here, it goes this way; hands there, it goes that way. Once you begin to feel the differences, you're on your way.

The essence of physical learning is developing distinctions, becoming aware of the differences between two actions and recognizing the consequences of each. This is the way we learn all basic activities—walking, running, even riding a bicycle—and the reason that we don't have to think about them once we learn them. Having mastered the "feel," we don't have to keep second-guessing ourselves. The best way to begin to develop this feel in golf is to swing in an exaggerated fashion, first in one way, then in the opposite way. Once these large differences are distinguished clearly, you can begin to move toward the more subtle ones.

Treat each shot as a new possibility—don't judge it. If you must evaluate your performance, rate the quality of your awareness. Use a 1 to 10 scale, where 1 is low awareness and 10 is high. I use many different "scorecards" in my teaching and this is one of them. These methods of scoring have one important difference from the normal method of scoring in golf: They are completely under your control. Whether it's awareness or, as I will talk about later, trust or courage, scoring "qualities" in this way creates a game that has tremendous value and that you can consistently win. Whereas your regular score will always be subject to the vagaries of weather and other factors you can't control, these other scores depend only on you.

SHADES OF MEANING

When you wear sunglasses the world looks darker. Have you ever had days when you've worn sunglasses so long that you forgot you had them on and started to think that the world really *was* darker than it is? Every culture is like a pair of glasses that colors the way you see the world. If you're not aware of the limitations of your culture—if you don't realize that you have glasses on—then you can see things only in a certain way. Only when you realize how the glasses shape your current point of view is it possible for you to develop a new point of view.

The Culture of Golfers causes people to see golf through a filter that says something is always wrong. It is based on the belief that somewhere there is a formula for success, and that golfers must continuously struggle to find it. But there is no freedom in formula. There is no satisfaction in feeling that something is wrong all the time. There is no joy in a continuous struggle against yourself. The only reason golfers put up with these things is because of the belief that they will lead to eventual success in golf, but it seems clear to me that for most people, that success is not happening. The Culture of Golfers is one way to see the golf world, but it is not the only way.

Once you become aware that you see golf (and likely other areas of your life, too) from the point of view that something is always wrong, change is possible. You can then move from a culture based on judgment to one based on possibility. This is the culture of extraordinary golf.

Chapter Four

CONCENTRATION

TIME TO THINK ABOUT IT

A few years ago I gave a workshop for thirty-five golf professionals in Hawaii. During one of my talks, I asked the group what they thought was the most important skill for developing an excellent golf game. After conferring among themselves, they settled upon concentration. I then asked how many of them teach concentration. No hands were raised. I asked how many of them had ever taken a lesson in concentration. Again, no response. I said, "Am I missing something here? We know how valuable this skill is, yet we don't know how to teach it and we don't know where to get a lesson in it!" There is no doubt that concentration is an immensely valuable skill, and there is no doubt that it can be taught and practiced. Let's start by asking the most basic question: What is concentration?

Concentration is the ability to focus your attention on that which you choose for as long as you choose. Most of us have minds that are continually hopping from one thing to another, focusing only briefly on each thing. It is possible to learn how to concentrate with greater intensity and for longer periods of time.

Golf demands a particular style of concentration that differs from that of many other sports. It's fair to say that anyone who can keep his or her mind focused for two or three seconds will be an excellent golfer. That doesn't sound so difficult, but it has been my experience that very few people can do it. Why? Simply because of the training. Through their practice, most golfers train themselves in a kind of concentration that is highly ineffective for play on the course. Let me show you how this training proceeds. I will talk about what occupies the mind in the second and a half to two seconds that it takes to swing a golf club.

SWING THOUGHTS

Throughout my early golfing years, I used to begin every swing with a key thought, no matter what club I was using. "Take it back slow," "Keep your head still," "Turn your shoulders"—you know what I'm talking about. As far as I could tell, every other golfer did the same, and I never questioned it. However, I came to realize that not only did these key thoughts change from day to day, they did not even last the extent of my swing. Whatever swing thought I had when I started, my backswing would be gone by the time of my follow-through. Sometimes it disappeared at the top of my backswing, sometimes at impact, sometimes at follow-through, but it never made it all the way through. I began to wonder about this.

One day I attended a seminar given by a well-known sports psychologist. In the question-and-answer period, I raised my hand: "We all start our golf swings with key swing thoughts, but we know they don't last throughout the swing. Plus, they often change from day to day. It seems we're putting our trust in something that we know we really can't depend on. Is there anything beyond key swing thoughts, something that we know will be there tomorrow, and next week? Something that we can rely on?" He looked at me and said, "You know, if you could ever answer that question, we'd both make a million bucks!" That was all he said.

When the seminar was over, I sat down and thought about what I had heard. According to the experts, my golfing future would consist of endless jumping from one key swing thought to another—always looking for a new one, always wondering how long my current one would last. I realized that I didn't want this. But I knew there must be something beyond swing thoughts; the game was much better than that. I began to look more deeply into what golfers really think about. I began to examine the nature of concentration.

I started by wondering what would happen if my mind didn't jump. I wanted to see if I could focus on a single thing throughout my swing, so I started with something very simple—the golf ball. I looked at the "T" on the Titleist that I was hitting and tried to keep looking at it as I swung. This was a simple task and I thought it would be easy for me, but it wasn't. When I swung, the ball would get blurry and waver, and often I couldn't see the "T" at all. This surprised me—why couldn't I just look at the ball? I began to understand that there was a tremendous amount going on in my mind as I swung the club, much more than I had ever realized. Fascinated, I continued with this exercise and many others.

As I learned more about the behavior of my own mind, I became curious to know if other golfers' behavior was similar. I started to question my students about their thoughts during the golf swing. This took a lot of time and persistence, since most golfers are not really aware of what they are thinking and experiencing during the swing. But a clear, consistent picture slowly began to emerge, and it's a real eye-opener.

JUMPING TO CONCLUSIONS

As I said earlier, the key thought typically covers only one facet of the swing. At the top of the backswing, by which time this first thought has usually run its course, something else happens. Most often this consists of visually reconfirming where the ball is and reconnecting with it—hit *that*. During the downswing the thoughts usually turn to anticipation of impact, and I have often seen this anticipation reflected in the faces of people whose swings I have filmed. After impact there is an immediate evaluation of the impact—good, bad, whatever—and finally the act of looking for the ball and evaluating its flight.

Let's go through this again: 1) key swing thought; 2) visual reconnection with ball; 3) anticipation of impact; 4) evaluation of impact; 5) evaluation of ball in flight. The average person has fully five different foci during the two seconds that it takes to complete the golf swing. I didn't just make this up. It comes from studying literally hundreds of people, observing them and asking them questions about their swing.

WHY YOU CAN'T TAKE IT WITH YOU

Average golfers practice hour after hour with these many thoughts. Then they step onto the first tee and ask

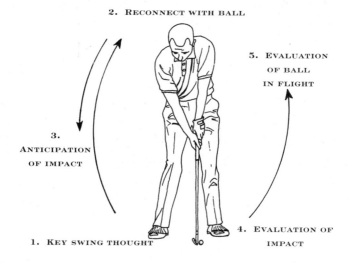

2. RECONNECT WITH BALL

5. EVALUATION
   OF BALL
   IN FLIGHT

3.
ANTICIPATION
OF IMPACT

1. KEY SWING THOUGHT

4. EVALUATION OF
   IMPACT

their minds to be clear, calm, and focused! Can't you see what a joke this is? They've been training their minds, day after day, to jump all over the place, and then they expect things to change completely when they start their round. But this isn't even the most extraordinary thing. What's really fascinating is that this mental jumping around can actually work on the practice tee. A golfer can go through the usual five-step process—jump, jump, hit, jump, jump—when practicing and achieve fine results. But this is devastating on the golf course.

I've had many, many people tell me that they find it very difficult to take their practice onto the golf course, that they leave their game on the practice tee. This is certainly understandable since they don't know what they're practicing, and they don't know what really works on the golf course. The fact that what works in one place won't work in the other is due to the differing conditions of practice and play.

Think of the thoughts that occur during the swing as pieces of cloth that have been stitched together. On the practice tee, the five thoughts that come to the typical golfer during the swing form a continuous piece of cloth, with the stitches holding tightly. But during an actual round, different, additional factors—the tension of actual play, the long time between shots—combine to put pressure on this tapestry of thoughts. I guarantee you that under these conditions the stitches will rip out at the places where you jump from thought to thought, and you will end up with gaps in between. These gaps are the danger spots.

In the gaps between thoughts where the stitching has come undone, fear, doubt, worry, and muscle-tightening come in. It's amazing what can happen in such a seemingly short amount of time. You start out with a key swing thought and take your backswing. At the top you change your focus and create a gap. Through this gap can come a thought like "Don't hit it to the left." You might then go into the filing cabinet of your mind, take out a recent image of hitting it to the left, bring that image into the present, imagine what hitting it left would feel like, evaluate it, react to it, and then start your downswing. All in an instant. What an amazing thing the human mind is!

CLOSE THE GAPS

Golfers with gaps in the swing are extremely vulnerable to fear and doubt. If you want any chance of freeing yourself from these gaps, I suggest you begin to practice a different style of concentration, one that is effective for golf. The question now is, What type of concentration is that? Let me return to the description of my concentration exercises, where I was trying to focus on the golf ball.

I stayed with this exercise, simply trying to see the golf ball clearly throughout my swing, and it became easier and easier. After a while I was able to stay with this one focus—watching the "T" on Titleist—for two seconds. To my delight, my play began to improve. I was very encouraged, so

2. RECONNECT WITH BALL

GAP

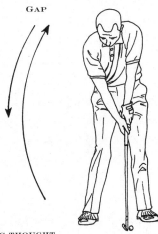

1. KEY SWING THOUGHT

I continued and shifted my focus to the club head. I wanted to see if I could keep my attention on the head of the club throughout all 540 degrees of arc—backswing, downswing, and follow-through.

This was also quite difficult at first. I realized that there were particular areas of my swing during which it was especially hard to maintain focus. (As I came to understand later, these blank spots are very significant, and I will discuss them further in the next chapter.) By staying with this exercise, I was eventually able to track the club head throughout my swing, and it made an enormous positive difference in my game. I continued in this pattern, focusing next on a part of my body, and then on the target, with similar results. From these experiences I began to draw some conclusions about the nature of concentration and the possibilities for golfers beyond key swing thoughts.

At the beginning of this chapter I said that concentration was the ability to focus your attention on one thing for a certain period of time. In the exercises I just described, I was able to achieve a high level of concentration on such things as the golf ball or the club head. Yet I was still able to hit golf shots, which means that I also had an awareness of the golf swing and the target. What this means, of course, is that there are levels of awareness and knowledge much deeper than those of the conscious mind. It is possible to concentrate fully on one thing, and yet still be able to do something else.

In these exercises, my ability to maintain a single focus benefited me in two ways. First, it helped me learn about the particular aspect on which I was focusing, and second, it removed self-interference and allowed me to play better. In addition to this, it was very enjoyable and gave me a sense of freedom I hadn't felt in a long time.

Most people think of concentration in terms of getting something, which you do—awareness and learning. But you must also give up something, and this can be hard for people. The swing thoughts and judgments that fill golfers' minds during the swing may seem like a lot of baggage, but it is familiar baggage and not so easy to get rid of. These thoughts can act like a safety net or a security blanket: If you don't have them, then what have you got? Nothing. You either have chatter, worry, doubts, and judgments, or you have nothing. Concentration is, in a sense, nothing. And nothing can help your golf game.

HERE, THERE, AND EVERYWHERE

Our lives are filled with inventions that allow us to keep our attention off what we are doing. We eat breakfast while watching television. We drive while listening to the radio and talking on a car phone. We run with headphones on and watch a game while working the StairMaster at the gym. And the content of what we see and hear reinforces this fragmenting of attention. The typical television commercial or MTV feature is nothing but jump, jump, jump, jump—completely analogous to the swing-thought situation I described earlier. The way we train our attention in what we consider normal life is the opposite of what is effective for golf. In the training section at the end of the book I describe specific exercises to help develop concentration, and in a way, these exercises will help counteract the training that we get from our day-to-day living.

One of the reasons that golf is so popular, I think, is that it requires a different pace and frame of mind than our regular lives. It's a refreshing change from what we get day to day. But the fact that society's training counteracts that of golf is a problem. This may be one of the reasons why statistics show that, over the years, improvements in golf performance have stagnated. The calm and focused state of mind that is necessary for good golf is hard to develop nowadays. But when it is achieved, it can have benefits that extend far beyond your golf game. I believe that the real purpose of games is to develop skills that will be useful in life, and golf is a perfect example. The ability to concentrate that you can develop through golf can be tremendously valuable in just about anything else you do. If all you get out of golf is an increased ability to concentrate, it will have been well worth it.

Chapter Five

INSTINCTIVE
KNOWLEDGE

TECHNIQUE AND POWER

In the thousands of golf lessons that I have given over the years, there have been three things that almost all students have told me they wanted: consistency, proper technique, and power. We'll talk about consistency later, so now let's look at technique and power. Everyone wants to hit the ball farther, even if they can already hit it a mile. And why not? It's a great feeling! Even though most golfers know that increased distance doesn't automatically lead to better scores, watching that ball fly a long way is a big part of the experience and enjoyment of the game.

There have been innumerable books written on power—I've read many and you probably have, too—and they all have their special approach, their special secret. Over the years I've tried many different methods, with mixed results. But through a combination of chance, persistence, and plain good fortune, my students and I have discovered a way to teach power and technique from a new point of view that has yielded remarkable results. Not only has it produced a dramatic increase in students' power, it has also led to insights that have opened up a whole new way of looking at the swing. Directing students in this particular exercise and seeing the amazement, delight, and transformation it produces in them and their swings has been a constant source of enjoyment for me and for the coaches I work with. Let me tell you how it all came about.

SERENDIPITY

One afternoon I was hitting a few balls at the range while waiting for my next lesson to begin. As I often do at times like this, I started fooling around with the club, just having fun and seeing what might happen. By chance I found that if I hit the ball and immediately let go of the club, the club would fly straight ahead about twenty yards. I did this a few times and it intrigued me, so I decided to try it with my next student, a man who had about a 25 handicap.

I asked him to hit the ball and release the club immediately after impact. He did so and the club flew almost directly to the left—the "hook" direction, since he was a right-handed golfer. Luckily, there were few other people on the range and it didn't interfere with anyone. As I retrieved the club I wondered why it had landed where it did. I asked him to try the exercise again and the same thing happened—directly left. I then tried to simplify things by saying, "Just throw the club straight after you hit the ball," but it didn't help. No matter how many times he tried, he couldn't get the club to go straight, yet I could, every time.

I realized that something interesting was going on here. My student was getting frustrated, so I told him not to put a ball on the tee, but simply to take a golf swing and throw the club straight ahead. This time the club went straight, and I noticed a change in his swing. It happened that I had a video camera sitting on a tripod, filming the whole thing. We rewound the tape and took a look at it.

When he was hitting the ball, his position through impact was that of a typical golfer: his body almost stopped, the club completely released. He sort of "snapped" at the ball, with the club moving hard to the left after impact. But when the ball was not there and he simply threw the club, a remarkable change took place. A remarkable and instantaneous change. Watching it on tape, I was amazed and exhilarated—something special was going on here. From that point on the club-throwing exercise became a part of my teaching process.

SCENE OF TRANSFORMATION

I will illustrate the wonderful things that happen during this exercise by describing one of my favorite workshop scenes—one that has been repeated many times but which I continue to find fascinating. It takes place in the late afternoon on the first day. Earlier in the day, the students

RICHARD, 10 HANDICAP:
REGULAR SWING
1. RICHARD'S BODY IS
LEANING TOWARD THE
TARGET AT THE TOP OF THE
BACKSWING. THE WEIGHT
SHIFT IS THE REVERSE OF
THAT WHICH PRODUCES
MAXIMUM POWER.

2. THE WRISTS ARE
COMPLETELY RELEASED
WELL BEFORE IMPACT. THE
BODY HAS ALREADY REACHED
THE SQUARE POSITION AND IS
BEGINNING TO STALL,
WAITING FOR THE HANDS TO
CATCH UP.

have done the club-throwing exercise with some old clubs I keep for this purpose. (I describe this in full detail in the exercise section of the book.) The other coaches and I have videotaped each student taking two swings. The first is their normal golf swing, and they hit a ball. The second—immediately after—is a swing with no ball present, and they simply throw the club straight ahead.

We gather in the meeting room to watch and discuss the videos, all twenty or so of us—typically about fifteen students and five coaches. The first person we take a look at is Richard—a forty-eight-year-old with a 10 handicap. Richard has played golf for thirty years—longer than any student in the group—and has tried everything he could

3. THE HANDS ARE WELL BEHIND THE BODY AT IMPACT AND THE CLUB IS SCOOPING THE BALL.

4. THE SCOOPING MOTION HAS CAUSED THE LEFT WRIST TO BUCKLE AND THE CLUB TO FLIP THROUGH IMPACT.

think of to achieve a consistent golf game. Yet by his own admission his game is erratic and often frustrating.

First I cue up his regular golf swing, and we play it a couple of times. Richard has a slightly better swing than the average golfer, but even he can see why it's not efficient or powerful: reverse weight pivot, club "thrown" from the top of the backswing, body stalling and a release of power before impact, club head "scooping" the ball. There he is on tape for all the world to see, and he's surprised (he wasn't aware of much of what he was doing), dismayed, and uncomfortable. His basic swing positions are shown above.

I go through Richard's swing point by point in front of the group, and it's an upsetting time for him. We talk about what it would take for him to improve, and I ask him what he would do first. He says, "I'd get my weight back." I ask him if he's tried that before. He says yes, but obviously it's had little effect. I ask what he would do next, and he says, "Delay the lag." I ask if he's tried that before, and he says yes, but to no avail. This pattern continues for a few more areas of his swing.

I finally look right at him and say: "If you've tried everything before and it hasn't worked, why should you expect anything to change at all? By your own admission, there are many things that are awkward and inefficient about your swing. Fixing all of them looks like a long and really difficult process." Richard now feels like he's stuck and sees nothing that can make any real difference in his game. He's really disheartened. He says, "I thought this was supposed to be a positive golf school. I feel really discouraged." He's at the point of breakdown, ready to give up on all the methods he's tried before. Cruel as it may seem, bringing him to this point is a necessary part of the process. This is a crucial moment in the exercise.

I then cue up the video of Richard throwing the club. I ask him: "Could you ever imagine yourself swinging like a golf pro?" His answer—"not really"—is typical of most golfers. I have found that very few people are capable of even imagining themselves doing extraordinary things, and thus resign themselves to mediocrity. I then ask Richard what position he would like to have at the top of his backswing.

As he describes his ideal position, I pause the club-throwing video at the backswing frame. His weight is set differently—instead of leaning toward the target, his body is coiled behind the ball. I say, "Something like that?" The light of amazement and enthusiasm comes into his eyes. "Yeah!" he says. "Like that!" Next I ask him what position he'd like to have at impact, and he says, "I'd really like to retain my wrist angle, and have my body moving with the club, not ahead of it or behind it." I stop the tape at the impact frame, and there it is. Richard, Mr.-10-Handicap-Slightly-Better-Than-Average-Golfer, looks like he belongs on the cover of a golf magazine.

He doesn't believe it, and you probably don't either, but there he is on the following pages.

MAGIC MOMENT

Richard just sits there, stunned, looking at his video. There's the swing he's always wanted, the one he never really thought he'd be able to do. He doesn't know what to say. The other students are equally surprised and amazed. A feeling—a spark—goes through the room. People realize that something extraordinary is happening, and they don't quite know how to react. They smile, shake their heads, chuckle—there's almost a giddy feeling in the air. It's a marvelous moment and a delight for me to be a part of. I play the tape a few more times to let it sink in.

Then I turn to Richard and ask him a question that is at the core of the whole learning process: "If you're already able to swing the way you want, what do we need to teach you?" From here we introduce the themes that will guide us over the next few days.

RICHARD, 10 HANDICAP: CLUB-THROWING SWING

HERE'S A REPEAT OF HIS REGULAR SWING:

The first two themes are these: 1) Your instincts are extraordinary, and basically you've gone against them from the time you first started golfing; 2) When Michelangelo created *David,* he went to a block of marble and removed everything that wasn't David—he added nothing; great golf is likewise a process of removing the interference you've put on yourself, almost from the very first day.

We all instinctively know how to propel an object in the most efficient way possible. If given time to experiment—without preconceived ideas of right and wrong—we will

feel our way toward the motion that provides us with our maximum power. Great golfers are people whose natural (club-throwing) swings are very similar to their regular swings. It is entirely possible that these excellent golfers play closer to their instincts than others. They don't constantly think, juggle, and adjust as much when they swing. They are much better able to step up to their shot and just let it go.

BASIC INSTINCTS

The club-throwing exercise provides a simple and direct way for people to get back in touch with their instincts. Richard is only the first of the students in the conference room to be discussed, and as we show the other videos the enthusiasm remains high. Whatever the golfer's age, gender, or handicap, the changes are remarkable. Some people's transformations are even more dramatic than Richard's. Here are a few more examples:

KAY, MEDIUM HANDICAP—REGULAR SWING

CLUB-THROWING SWING

I have hundreds of videos similar to these, and the evidence for the effectiveness of the club-throwing swing is overwhelming. There is an extraordinary difference between most golfers' regular swings and their far more fluid, efficient, and powerful club-throwing swings. But the objective in golf is to propel not the club forward, but the golf ball, which leads to the obvious, $64,000 question: What is it that makes the difference?

In looking at the videos, the only consistent visible difference is where people's eyes look before they start the

swing. In the regular swing, their eyes are on the golf ball, as if to say, "I'm going to hit *that*." In the club-throwing swing, their eyes look forward, as if to say, "I'm going to throw it out *there*." On the video this looks like a small matter, but it makes all the difference in the world. The club-throwing swing is superior to the regular swing primarily because of this one thing: the target was changed from the golf ball to the hole.

ZACH, MEDIUM HANDICAP—REGULAR SWING

CLUB-THROWING SWING

DECEPTION IN PERCEPTION

From practically the first time we played, most of us, in a sense, have been hoodwinked into believing that the golf ball is the target. And interestingly enough, the resulting swing is concurrent with this belief. The lifting up on the backswing, the reverse weight shift, the fully released hands at impact—all the things that look so awkward and unnatural to golfers watching their videos in fact seem quite rea-

sonable if you assume that getting the club face square to the ball at impact is the ultimate objective, which it is for most people. The body's instincts are very wise and they will do whatever best achieves the given objective. We just need to be aware of what objective we give them.

I have a video of two young men, both baseball players, on the driving range. One is also a golfer, and he wants to teach the game to his friend, who has never swung a club before. The novice takes his first swing and completely misses the ball, but he has a wonderfully full and powerful

SUSAN, HIGH HANDICAP—REGULAR SWING

CLUB-THROWING SWING

swing, with great hand and body position through the impact area. He then takes a second swing, also with a good position, and hits a short slice. His buddy starts talking to him. I don't know exactly what is said, but I have a pretty good idea: head down, left arm straight, shift the weight, etc.—we all know the tune. On the third swing the beginner's body stops at impact, he casts the club at the ball, he has an awkward position in terms of what his instincts tell him, and he hits the ball straight about 150 yards. His buddy turns to him and says, "Now you've got it!"

It has taken only three swings for this person to go completely against what he instinctively knows to be true, this in order to survive in the golf environment—at least in the environment that was presented to him. I think this is what happens to most of us from the very beginning.

In the club-throwing exercise we change the target to what it really is in golf—out *there*. The ball is simply something that the swing passes through on its way toward the target. And with the new target, the body's instincts hold true. The resulting swing matches exactly what is necessary

JIM, HIGH HANDICAP—REGULAR SWING

CLUB-THROWING SWING

to produce the maximum force to propel an object forward. The body and arm positions change, the head and
feet are in a different place, the weight is set in a new way.
Everything changes, and remarkably, it changes all at once,
not in the piecemeal way that most people think is the
norm. Contrary to most current teaching beliefs, I have
seen strong evidence for golf learning to be an all-at-once
phenomenon.

TO BE IS TO DO

When we finish showing the videos, the room is electric. The students have seen possibilities in their swings that they never thought existed, and they're raring to go. I repeat the basic question, this time to the entire group: "If you can already swing like that, what do you need to do tomorrow when you practice?" The answers I get are instructive and crucial in understanding what it takes to sustain such breakthroughs.

MY REGULAR SWING

RICHARD'S CLUB-THROWING SWING

One person says, "I'll try to pull my arms down into that position before impact." Another replies, "I'll try to turn away on the backswing." A third simply states, "I'll try to swing like I'm throwing the club." These seem like reasonable suggestions, but none of them will make a real difference in their swings. Techniques like these are nothing more than swing keys, "tips" such as these golfers have all tried many times before with no lasting success. They are the legacy of the old Culture of Golfers, the mind-set that sees the swing as a fragile mechanism always in need of

fixing. They will produce nothing more than the ordinary up-again, down-again results with which we are all too familiar.

What changed the swing was not "doing" something different. This is the most important point of the entire exercise and of all my teaching. The changes came about because of a new point of view, essentially a new way of "being." Given the new point of view, the actions changed naturally, smoothly, and all at once, not piece by piece. Let me repeat, with emphasis: *Extraordinary changes come from a new point of view—a new way of being.* In this, as in all aspects of the game, "being" precedes "doing."

As the videos so clearly show, the body behaves according to the target—the point of view—that we give it. If the target is the ball, the body will often lift up on the backswing, since the most efficient windup turns away from the target, and up, in this case, is away from the target on the ground. With this target, the wrists will be fully released before impact, since this is their objective point. When the target is changed to the flagstick, the same instincts hold true, and the body's actions change naturally.

Almost all golfers work from the opposite direction. They focus first on the endless details of the swing, which are actually the results of other things. They treat the secondary events as if they were primary and are often unaware of the real primary causes. This process—and I know it well—is time-consuming and erratic, and rarely satisfying. The details cannot be ignored, of course, but in their proper perspective they are much easier to understand and manage.

Let me use an analogy here that any parent will appreciate. Imagine you have a house full of young children and you want to get them all out the door. One way to do this is to go around the house rounding them up one by one and pointing them in the right direction. But young kids have short attention spans, and you know what will happen with this method. They will be distracted constantly and you'll have to run around like a sheepdog to keep them heading the right way. You can do it—usually—but it's a lot of work. However, another method (which unfortunately you can't use very often in real life) is much simpler and more efficient. You go to the freezer, grab a carton of ice cream, walk to where you want the kids to go, and yell, "Ice cream!" In a few seconds you'll be surrounded.

The first method is the way most golfers approach their swing. They try to get the ball going in the right direction by putting all their energy into manipulating the details and the mechanics of the swing. There are a lot of pieces to attend to, and the mind, like children, is easily distracted. It ends up being a difficult and not very satisfying job. The second method, of course, corresponds to changing the golfing target.

BREAKING THROUGH

My definition of a breakthrough is the moment that truly alters a person's perception. It's when the light bulbs go on and you really get it. By any measure, the club-throwing exercise is a true breakthrough for most people. There are two main reasons why it has such a powerful effect.

The first is that it shows people they have strong natural instincts for golf. The great majority of golfers see themselves as awkward and unnatural when they play ("something's always wrong"), and believe that graceful, fluid swings are the property of a lucky few. And most golfers feel awkward when they play since, as I said before, almost all of us have gone against our instincts.

When people feel themselves complete an efficient, powerful swing, and then see the evidence on video, their self-images begin to change in a significant way. If you believe yourself to be an average, fairly awkward golfer, how can you hope to sustain extraordinary play? However, if you see yourself as someone who can produce a graceful, powerful swing, you have a whole new world of possibilities. The club-throwing exercise goes beyond mere positive thinking and gives people the actual experience of swinging in a new and exciting way.

The second reason this exercise works well is that the club-throwing swing is so dramatically different from the normal swing. As I said earlier and will continue to say throughout this book, the key to learning is to be aware of differences. The club-throwing swing is such a far cry from most people's norm that most golfers can feel the differences immediately.

So it stands to reason that all you have to do is toss clubs until you get them flying straight and long, then tee it up and you're on your way, right? The folks at the home course won't believe it's the same you! Ah, yes. Wouldn't it be nice!

On the surface, it really does seem that easy. I recently gave a seminar for both professionals and amateurs in Palm Springs. When the professionals saw both sets of their videos, they were not particularly impressed since, as I explained, a professional's two swings are close to the same. But when the pros saw the amateurs' different swings, they were blown away. They reacted the same way I did during the very first lesson in which I saw a club-throwing swing: "Why don't they just keep swinging like *that?*" Why not indeed?

Achieving breakthroughs is one thing, sustaining them is quite another. Most of us have experienced the first, a lot fewer of us the second. We all know the feeling of days when we think we've reached another level of play, only to come crashing back to earth a short time later, when the magic of the latest secret seems to have worn off. In the club-throwing exercise, students see what they do now, and they see what else is possible. But how do they get from one to the other? That's the fascinating part of my job. It's an endless challenge that produces endless surprises. The club-throwing swing was a wonderful surprise, and it gets even better.

NATURAL TIMING

People often tell me that if they could just get inside the body of a certain favorite professional golfer and experience a great golf swing, it would make a real difference in their game. We're undoubtedly moving toward the day when that will be possible. The way technology is developing, I'm sure a time will come when you will be able to get inside a suit of some kind, program it for the professional you want (FC for Fred Couples, PS for Patty Sheehan, and so forth), and "swing like a pro"—for a fee, of course. Fascinating as this may sound, I don't think it would do much to improve people's golf swings.

If there is one thing that all human beings agree on, it's that each of us is unique. There has never been another you and there never will be. So why should we continually try to imitate someone else's golf swing? If we are truly unique, then we should each have a unique swing—a particular way of moving the club that is the most efficient and powerful for our body and no one else's. Doesn't it stand to reason that this would be the only swing we could "own," the only one that we could really trust? Certainly we should look to others' swings as an aid in learning, but only in the same way that we look to our parents' speech when we're learning to talk as children—we look for the basic idea, then we make it our own.

The club-throwing exercise, I believe, allows people to experience their natural swing. This is the swing that your body, in all its wisdom, knows is the most efficient and powerful. This is your instinctive swing; in a sense, it's a part of who you are. This is the swing that you know will always be there. This is the swing that you do when you don't think about it, when you don't get in your own way. Either you have self-interference, or you have this natural golf swing. Through further analysis of students' videos, I have found that this self-interference is clearly visible. Let me explain.

THE TIMING IS RIGHT

Late one evening after the first day of a workshop, I was at home reviewing the videos we had shot that afternoon, preparing for the next day's work. As I noticed the differences between the club-throwing swings and the regular swings, it suddenly occurred to me that in addition to giving pictures of swing positions, the video camera could also serve as an accurate timer. I had always been aware of different timings between the two swings, and here at last was a way to see those differences clearly. I began to time the different parts of the swings, counting the frames of the backswings, the downswings, and the follow-throughs. And what I saw amazed me.

Videotape runs at a constant thirty frames per second, each frame thus representing 1/30th of a second. In a typical student's regular swing, the backswing took about thirty frames, the downswing about nine frames, and the follow-through about seventeen frames. Yet in the club-throwing swing, the numbers were quite different: twenty-six for backswing, thirteen for downswing, and twelve for follow-through.

These discrepancies are remarkable. In the typical student's regular swing, backswing-to-downswing ratio was approximately 3 to 1. But in the club-throwing swing—the instinctive, natural swing—the ratio was only about 2 to 1. Quite a change!

And look what else these numbers tell us. The regular swing takes a longer time to go back, a shorter time to get

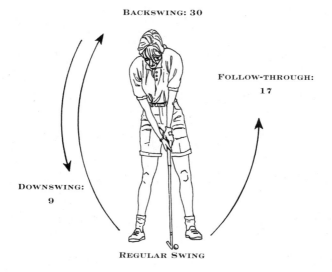

BACKSWING: 30

FOLLOW-THROUGH: 17

DOWNSWING: 9

REGULAR SWING

down to the ball, and a longer time to follow through. While it appears that the club is traveling faster through the ball, in fact it only starts out quicker, and is actually slowing down through the ball, as evidenced by the longer time it takes to follow through. In the club-throwing swing, the club starts down slower, but accelerates through the ball, and so has a much quicker follow-through. This matches the visual evidence: The regular swing typically has a tentative, overcontrolled, off-balance backswing; a quick, early release; and a stalling of the body and club through the impact area.

The difference between the two timings is created by self-interference. In the club-throwing swing, the student is simply given an objective. Without detailed instructions on how to reach it, the student lets his or her body figure it

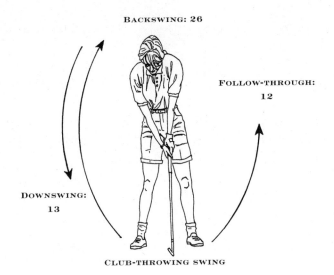

BACKSWING: 26

FOLLOW-THROUGH: 12

DOWNSWING: 13

CLUB-THROWING SWING

out. The resulting swing is easy, powerful, and consistent. We always film at least three or four swings of each type per student, and the club-throwing swings are almost always, in form and timing, exactly the same. When you don't have to think about it, you can do it over and over again.

The regular swing is a different story. When the golf ball is there, the whole self-interference package—the hopes, worries, and fears; the thoughts on how-to and how-not-to; the woulds, the coulds, and the shoulds—is there too. The resulting swing not only varies dramatically from the natural swing, but it varies in an inconsistent way—the three or four regular swings usually differ from each other in form and timing. When you get in your own way you mess yourself up, and you do it a little bit differently each time.

THE SURE WAY IS YOUR WAY

This evidence makes it clear to me that each person has an ideal golf swing, one that is unique and has a unique timing. Interestingly enough, this natural timing exists on all types of swings, not just the full swing.

I have recently begun filming students' chipping and putting strokes in the same way—first hitting a regular shot with a ball, then taking the ball away and throwing the club. Much to everyone's amusement—the students really get a kick out of this—the pattern is the same.

Each student's club-throwing swings are very consistent and—whether chips, putts, or full swings—have a similar backswing-to-downswing ratio. Each student's regular swings have much more variation, with ratios far different from those of the club-throwing swings. And here's another interesting point: The stroke that a student is most comfortable with is almost always the one that is closest to the natural swing. If a student describes him- or herself as a good putter, for example, the regular timing of that particular stroke will be very close to its natural timing.

The lesson is clear: Don't try to imitate someone else's swing and timing; look for your own. How do you do this? Through awareness, which is what this book is all about. But a word of caution: I've done some swing analysis here, complete with specific numbers. This process can be very helpful, but it can also be dangerous. This is a point where the Culture of Golfers, with its focus on fixing details, will often try to come in and take over. The Culture of Golfers thrives on data, and swing positions and numbers make it lick its chops. There might be a tendency to take these numbers, interpret them literally, and apply them directly to your swing. You might want to time your swing and try to make it closer to the 2-to-1 ratio (just an example) that I mentioned . You might want to try a specific cadence when you swing, or something similar—we all know what these tendencies are. Please, restrain yourself.

The important thing to remember, and what we emphasize to students on the second day of the workshop, is that you can't figure out how to do this. No one really knows how to swing a golf club. The amount of muscle movement involved is far beyond the type of understanding that we often feel we need to have. You can't figure out how to do it, but you *can* do it. It's the experience that counts. You must realize that understanding is the lowest step on the way to learning—it's the booby prize. Understanding may lead to experience, but it has little value in and of itself.

What my colleagues and I work to develop in students is a baseline of awareness. Every student is aware of certain parts of the swing, but only certain parts. The video analysis helps us fill in the gaps.

KNOWING WHAT YOU DON'T KNOW

In an earlier chapter I said that the one thing common to all my many video sessions was that every student was surprised by his or her swing. Each person, without exception, was completely in the dark about certain areas of the swing. Filling in the blind spots is what it's all about, and the video analysis helps us see exactly where those spots are. Even if we were to be able to get inside a professional's swing, we would still have the same blind spots and the same swing problems. If we can't be awake in our own swing, how can we be more alert in someone else's?

The blind spots are the areas of the regular swing where the timing is most discrepant with that of the natural swing. These spots can occur anywhere in the swing, so let me give an example from the most common area, the beginning of the downswing. In a typical club-throwing swing, it takes about eight frames for the hands to go from the top of the backswing to hip level. In the regular swing, it can take as few as four frames. When the ball is present, golfers typically rush the beginning of the downswing such that they have no idea where the club really goes. Because of the speed and lack of awareness, the path of the club is erratic. When golfers become aware of the club again, near the bottom of the downswing, they try to make corrections, but these are usually too late.

The point of the video analysis is not to identify the natural swing and try to imitate it. That is the outside-in approach of the Culture of Golfers. The point is to determine the areas of most need—the blind spots—and focus the awareness exercises on these areas. This approach illuminates one of the main reasons why golf teaching can often be frustrating and ineffective.

Most swing problems occur in the blind spots. Yet when people want to fix a problem, they look only in the areas of which they are aware. They can't look in the blind spots because they don't even know that the blind spots exist! Can you see the absurdity of it? It's as if they are car mechanics who know only about carburetors. Every time they try to fix their car, they look at the carburetor for the problem, since that's all they know. Sometimes they fix the problem, but most often not. They are often frustrated and the car . . . well, it always seems to need work.

As the video shows, the same blind spots occur in each

type of swing. If a golfer has a blind spot at the beginning of the downswing in the full swing, he or she will have a similar blind spot when chipping or putting. Accordingly, increasing your awareness of a blind spot in one type of swing can help all your swings. The more you fill in the blanks in your putting stroke, for example, the more it will help your full swing—and chipping—and vice versa. When you work on anything, you work on everything.

DON'T FIGHT YOURSELF

The path of awareness leads you toward your instincts. It leads you toward the things you do naturally. In a very real way, it leads you toward yourself—toward who you really are.

Once you begin to get in touch with your instincts, you begin to realize the folly of trying to go against them. It became very clear to me as a result of these exercises that you cannot have consistent technique unless it is based on natural timing. In other words, if your natural downswing takes fourteen frames, and your regular downswing takes nine frames, your club will never find the most efficient and powerful path when you hit a ball. It will almost always take an outside route and release early, since that is the only way it can get to the ball in nine frames. Yet another problem of traditional teaching is that it tries to teach golf technique without improving timing or even being aware that it is way off.

As I said at the beginning of this chapter, this discovery process based on the club-throwing exercise is a continual delight to me and my associates. When people realize that they have a natural swing and a natural timing, they are amazed. It is a truly extraordinary moment, almost as if a switch is being flipped: lights out for the Culture of Golfers and "something's always wrong," lights on for natural instincts and a whole new world of possibilities.

INTERLUDE: WE'VE GOTTA HAVE IT

I think it would be a good idea to take a short break here and reflect for a moment on how most people try to learn golf. Let me start by telling you another story from my Peace Corps days in Africa.

I had taken a brief vacation and was hitchhiking back into Ghana from the neighboring country of Togo. I had a few more days before I needed to return to my village and resume teaching. I was heading to the office of the Swiss ambassador, an enthusiastic golfer whom I had contacted through a friend. The ambassador had agreed to trade a round of golf for some lessons, and we had an appointment that morning.

I found a ride and was cruising along happily toward the capital city of Accra, looking forward to a day of golfing. However, as we passed the airport several tanks suddenly pulled into the road and started shooting over the tops of the cars. All at once military planes appeared in the sky, dropping bombs over the city. Mortar fire and machine-gun fire exploded all around. The whole city basically erupted.

All the traffic was now heading out of the city, and with good reason. But I had nowhere to go in this direction, so the only thing I could think to do was continue on my way. I got out of the car and started hiking into the city toward the embassy, chaos all around me. I passed an open window and heard a voice speaking over a shortwave radio—the voice of the general who was staging this coup. He announced that the president had been captured and parliament disbanded. He urged everyone to put down their arms. The firing continued.

I picked my way through the streets and alleys past roving bands of troops. I had a few close calls—none were too close, luckily. I finally got to the embassy and knocked on the door. I had no idea what I was going to say. Someone jerked open the door and said, "What? What do you want?" Behind him things were in complete disarray. I said that I had come to see the ambassador. He asked, "What for?" I couldn't think of a good answer, so I said, "Recreational reasons." He was shocked. "For *what?*" "For golf," I finally replied.

He was about to shut the door in my face when the ambassador, who happened to be close by, stuck his head around the corner. He said, "Are you Mr. Shoemaker, the golf pro?" I said yes. "Come with me." He took me into his room, sat me down, then left. I waited for twenty minutes.

The chaos continued. I heard people trying to get Zurich on the telex, but the telex was down. No one knew who was in control of the government. For everyone in this office, the world was falling apart.

I was feeling very uncomfortable, thinking, "What the heck am I doing here?" Suddenly the ambassador walked in and shut the door behind him. He walked over to an umbrella stand and grabbed an umbrella. Then he walked up to me, took a golfer's stance, and said: "Mr. Shoemaker, you must help me. I have ze shanks!"

For the next twenty minutes we worked on what he could do to cure the shanks.

HOOKED

Amazing but true. Even though his world was in shambles, the ambassador couldn't pass up a chance to make a difference in his golf game. The game even took precedence over things that were not only significant, but urgent. This is obviously an extreme example, but such obsession is not at all uncommon. What is it about games that we feel is so important, that hooks us so deeply? And why do we feel such an urgency to "get it" and get it now?

Through this book I hope to open your eyes to new and exciting possibilities in golf and show you fresh, new ways to learn it and play it. I would like nothing more than to increase your enthusiasm for the game and make you eager to try out these ideas. I know from experience that most people find this last chapter on technique and power—which I feel makes a genuine breakthrough—particularly fascinating, and those who become aware of it immediately want to go out and toss a few clubs. If this is the case with you, terrific!

But what I'm after here is genuine, lasting improvement in your golf game, and that doesn't happen overnight. We live in a fast-paced, impatient society where instant gratification is often the norm. When we want something, we want it now! This sense of urgency is certainly reflected in our approach to games, especially golf. Yet it is another case in which the conditioning of our society counteracts what is necessary for success in golf. Even though sudden, dramatic improvement does happen—and I have seen it in many of my students—in the long run, the "gotta have it now" attitude just doesn't work. On an unrealistically performance-oriented timetable, the wonderful initial enthusiasm for a new idea can often turn sour. There's enough discouragement and frustration going on in the golf world, and I don't want to add to it.

As my story about the Swiss ambassador illustrates, games are important to us. There's no sense in pretending that they're not. Even though golf may seem ludicrous from another's perspective, when we play it we care about the game, and we care how we do. Since games are important to us, why not give them proper time and attention?

As long as you play golf, there will be a relationship between you and the game itself. The kind of relationship you have and how you view it will greatly affect your learning, performance, and enjoyment of the game.

POPPING THE QUESTIONS

The real questions about your relationship with golf are those that will be somewhat familiar to all of us: Is this just an affair or do you really care about the game? Are you involved only for what you can quickly get out of it, or are you willing to put in time and effort to make the relationship work? These questions may seem a little silly, but in fact they make a lot of sense, and your answers will have a big effect on your game.

In my case, I started out with a genuine love for the game, then lost it for a while. During my twenties, the performance aspect—what golf could do for me to make me look good—took over and the relationship turned into an affair. But now, happily, I'm back in love with the game— all of it. I love the feel of the club in my hand and the grass under my feet. I love the sights and smells of the course. I love playing, but I also love practicing and teaching. I love the whole thing. I intend to be with the game for a long time, so I'm interested in methods and ideas that will help me achieve real growth and improvement, no matter how long it takes. And the wonderful thing is, with this attitude it doesn't take so long.

This approach to the game can work no matter what

your involvement with golf is. For some people golf is a real passion—their "spouse," as it were. For others, golf is more casual, like a good friend. But the basic principles of the relationship are the same. Even though you don't see a friend as often as a spouse, you still show her or him similar care, attention, and kindness. That is, if you are interested in maintaining the relationship.

As I mentioned in the beginning of this book, to get the most out of what I say here you need to broaden your perspective—instead of reading small, read big. That advice certainly applies in this chapter. In your relationship with golf, take the long view. Make it deep, make it solid. The game is worth it, and so are you.

Chapter Six

COACHING

When people think or talk about golf teachers they usually focus on the particular method, or "system," that the teachers use. Each system has its own technical approach, its own training regimen, and often its own special, patented training aids as well. These systems are frequently named for the teachers who create them, further strengthening the identification between the teacher and the content of the teaching.

In this chapter I would like to take a different look at teaching—a different point of view. Instead of focusing on the technical content—the "what"—I would like to focus on the identity of the teacher and the process of teaching itself—the "who" and "how." The terms *teaching* and *coaching* are similar, but they have important differences. To describe what my associates and I do, I prefer to use the term *coaching*, for reasons I will explain.

This chapter is divided into three parts. The first concerns my basic philosophy of coaching, how to become your own coach, and how to coach others to coach you. The second part is about coaching a person who is close to you—spouse, friend, lover—and the unique problems associated with this often difficult task. The third part expands on the second, focusing on parent-child coaching.

A. WHAT IS COACHING?

To most people, a golf teacher is someone who has played the game for a long time, who plays better than the student, and who has a particular technical method that has been proven to result in lower scores. The teacher's job is first to teach the system to the student, then to make sure that the student stays with the system when things go wrong—initial instruction, then constant tune-up. In short, to most people a golf teacher is a person who tells you what to do.

In the chapter on awareness and learning I talked about the Culture of Golfers, in which the dominant philosophy is that something is wrong with the swing and must be fixed. In this view the teacher is the fixer and provides the outside knowledge necessary for improvement. Extraordinary golf turns this process inside out, so the role of teacher must be similarly reversed.

As you may know, the word "educate" comes from the Greek meaning "to lead forth." Its original connotation was helping to bring out that which was inside—working from the inside out. It does not mean "to fill up," which has a sense of going outside in. In traditional golf teaching, the emphasis is on outside in. The golf teacher is like a gas station, a place where you fill the tank that gets you started, and the place you revisit whenever you run dry. This way of teaching works to an extent, but it is, in my opinion, ordinary, and we're talking extraordinary here. I'd like to show you a different possibility.

REFLECTIONS

As I have said, the first step to real improvement in golf is increased awareness of your swing—putting and chipping as well as the full swing—and I believe that helping you achieve that awareness is a golf coach's primary role. If you think back to previous chapters, in particular the one on power and timing, it is clear that the innate abilities of each golfer are really extraordinary. The genius resides in the student, not in the coach. The coach's primary job is to help the student become aware of that genius and remove the barriers that hinder it. A successful coaching session ends with the student trusting him- or herself more than the coach.

The student-coach relationship is similar to that of Sherlock Holmes and Dr. Watson. In the Conan Doyle stories, Watson's feedback would help the great detective clarify his thoughts, but it was Holmes who made the actual discoveries. Similarly, the golf coach helps the student get in touch with the experiences through which the student will discover greater awareness. In essence, I believe that the ideal coach acts as a clear, nonjudgmental mirror that reflects what really happens when you swing a club. Rather than "teach" you, which suggests showing you something you didn't know, he or she "coaches" you—helps you bring out and strengthen the instinctual knowledge you already have. A coach believes in the learning abilities of the student and is committed to helping the student get the most out of those abilities.

I consider myself and my associates to be coaches, and we work on being that clear, unbiased mirror. Of course we also guide, explain, demonstrate, focus, encourage, and show possibilities, but the heart of our interaction with students is providing feedback that will help them develop an awareness of what they actually do. This is a simple process, but it is hard to perform well. There are a variety of obstacles, the first being the judgments that are all too easy to make.

When you make judgments, you don't see what is there, rather you see what you think should be there. Making a judgment means, among other things, that you have removed your attention from the present in order to recall the idealized image to which the comparison (judgment) is being made. Complete awareness requires that you keep your attention fully focused on the present; any judgments that you make will cause gaps in the overall picture. These are the same types of "blind spots" that I described earlier in the chapter about power, and that are so apparent when golfers see videos of their swings. Coaches can have them as well as students.

The mirror that gives the truest reflection is clear and

smooth. A mirror that is clouded or bent will give a distorted view, as in a carnival fun house. Striving to be ideal mirrors, my associates and I continually work at being aware of things that might obscure or distort the reflections we give. Judgments are the most common of these, but there are others as well.

In traditional golf instruction the teacher is seen as the giver of knowledge, a view that usually gives him or her superiority in a hierarchical relationship with the student. The respect this position commands can be a real trap for the teacher. It's an easy role to fall into with all the attention and admiration you get, yet it is hard to get out of. It is difficult to change your mind or admit that something isn't working when you're expected to have all the right answers. And dependencies inherent in this relationship can be addictive. It's easy for the teacher to operate—often unconsciously—so as to keep the student coming back. The teacher-as-knowledge-giver approach can create a major distortion in the ideal coaching mirror.

The third most common problem area concerns the focus, or agenda, of the instruction session. Since traditional teaching is based on a standardized system that the student must learn, this agenda is often set by the teacher. In contrast, the ideal coaching approach is to have the agenda set by the student. A partner of mine, Garry Lester, recently led a workshop on coaching during which he asked, "What is a coach?" A youngster in the back stood up and replied, "A coach is a person who knows what you want and helps you get it." I heartily agree. The key to coaching is knowing what the student wants. A coach is a person who listens to and honors a student's values, goals, and commitments, and builds the instruction session around them. This philosophy is the cornerstone of coaching. It's easy to give people what you want to give them, rather than what they want and need. As coaches we need to constantly make sure the agendas are appropriate for the students.

NO MODELS

Most golf instruction uses an ideal model—a formula—as a basis of comparison. When I give workshops for other coaches, I am often asked if it is possible to coach someone without using a model. In reply I ask how it feels to coach based on a standard formula. The dialogue typically proceeds in the following way:

"I like having the answers. It makes me feel like I know what I'm doing and that I'm giving students their money's worth."

"Is that all you feel?"

"Well, actually it can be pretty boring."

"Why?"

"Because I'm basically saying the same things over and over again. Every lesson is alike and I don't feel that I'm learning much myself."

"How does it feel at the end of the day?"

"At first I was okay, but I've noticed that lately I get pretty exhausted. I don't enjoy it as much as I used to."

"I understand. I used to teach that way myself. Let's consider a different approach. Let's say it was possible for you to constantly learn from your students. How would you act with a student if you knew that this person might give you an insight that could transform your life and your ability to coach?"

"I'd be pretty interested."

"Do you think this could happen, given the way you are coaching now?"

"Probably not."

"Do you think you might have to give up your current coaching formulas for this to happen?"

"Well, I guess so, but that would be hard to do. How do you teach without a model? How do you tell students what they're supposed to do?"

It is risky to coach without having the answers, especially when someone is paying you money and expects you to be an expert. But if you believe, as my colleagues and I do, that the genius resides in the student, why would you want to give this genius the answers? Like Watson with Holmes, you're there to help in the discovery and be amazed. How can you do this? Let me illustrate by describing the beginning of a typical lesson of mine. After the student and I introduce ourselves and get to know each other a bit, the conversation usually goes somewhat like this:

"You've invested time, energy, and money in this lesson. What would you like to get out of it?"

"Well, I guess I'd just like to improve my game."

"Okay. But if this lesson were to be extraordinary and give you something of real value, what would it be? When you leave this lesson, what would you like to have gotten from it that would make it really worth your time?"

"I've always had this slice, and for once I'd like to get rid of it."

"Getting rid of a slice is one thing, but that's no guarantee it won't come back. Wouldn't it be better to find out how you slice, and also how to hook, and the difference between the two? If you learn how to curve the ball, don't you think it would be easier to hit it straight?"

"That sounds great."

"Okay. So if you leave this lesson able to feel the difference between a slice, a hook, and hitting it straight, would that be enough?"

"Yes, I'd like that."

"Good. But if you start getting concerned with distance or anything else that gets us off the subject, do I have your permission to come back to this goal?"

"Yes."

"Terrific! So let's go find out how you slice. . . ."

This dialogue has accomplished several key things. Most important, it has established a commitment. In my opinion, there can be no coaching without a commitment. We have also constructed an envelope of expectations and a time frame. Student and coach have joined together in the discovery process, with each responsible for his or her role. With this beginning, the lesson has a real possibility of success.

REVIEW

Let me recap. The key to learning is awareness, and the action-awareness-result feedback loop is the process by which all deep physical learning takes place. The coach's role is to help increase that awareness, and the most effective coach functions as a mirror from which students get clear, unbiased feedback on what it is they are actually doing. There are many things that can affect the coach and distort the mirror, the main ones being judgments (right way/wrong way), hierarchical relationships (teacher as knowledge-giver), and personal or teaching-system preferences (teacher sets agenda). The coach is aware of the student's goals, values, and commitments and uses these to shape the session.

Once communication between student and coach is established and the agenda set, the coach-student interaction should consist of the following: The student performs an action and says, "I was aware that I did this," and the coach responds, "I observed that you did that." It's really that simple.

Now, I know from experience that your reaction to this is likely to be skepticism. It can be hard to believe that something that looks so simple and easy can be so effective.

We all tend to expect more from instruction sessions—more structure, more data, more stuff that we can work on. We have been conditioned to think that that's what learning is about. Believe me, I often hear a similar voice in my head when I'm coaching. There is a part of all of us that wants to control things, do more, make things happen. But think about your own instances of extraordinary play and descriptions you've read of others'. Isn't the dominant experience one of *not* controlling, of trusting yourself and letting go? Coaches also need to let go and trust themselves and the learning process. My associates and I are continuously working on the same issues as our students, and we see this parallel experience as a key factor in keeping our coaching vital and effective.

Here's a fanciful example that will help illustrate my points. Imagine that you were a fourth-grade teacher many years ago, and the young Albert Einstein was in your class. You realized that he had an enormous capacity for learning, and you knew what he was going to become. How would you treat him? Would you fill him with data and make him memorize lots of rules? Or would you question and inspire, develop and draw out? Would you try to fill him up or try to help him grow?

All human beings possess an amazing and highly developed learning system, the product of millions of years of evolution. We're just beginning to learn about this system and just beginning to be able to really communicate with it. A coach is a person who recognizes this system, honors it, and is committed to making it work.

PROCESS

This may not be the most common philosophy of coaching, but I believe it is the most effective. The subject fascinates me, and the deeper I delve into it, the more interesting it gets. Now let's see how this point of view can make a difference in the way you learn and/or coach the game.

The well-known KISS rule (Keep It Simple . . .) is a good one to follow here because the essential action is quite simple. When you're practicing—coaching yourself—focus on being aware of what you're doing and of the results your actions produce. (The chapter on awareness and learning and its associated exercises cover this in more detail.) This book is really about coaching yourself. It's based on the simple premise of asking, "What was I aware that I did?" and then asking, "What did I actually do?" until the answers are the same.

It helps to have an extra pair of eyes for this process, and that's where coaching others to coach you comes in. Again, the basic interaction is simple: You say what you experienced, the other person says what he or she saw. Just about anyone can help you with this, and I often find that it works better with someone who doesn't know the game very well; that person is less likely to give judgments and suggestions that could cloud the mirror. The goal is for the other person simply to reflect what he or she sees.

But as I discussed earlier, this simple action is not all that easy to perform. People are not by nature objective observers. We all have our own ideas and opinions. Especially in a golf coaching situation, we have a real desire to help someone out, to give something to someone else—something more than just a report of what he or she did. On top of this there is the relationship that always exists between two people working together, with its emotional and psychological ramifications.

All these factors can combine to make the simple action not so simple. Since I work with this type of interaction every day, I have a lot of experience dealing with the problems that come up. Over the years I've developed a set of ground rules that, if followed, seem to greatly increase the chances for a successful, satisfying coaching situation. These three rules are best explained in context. The following scenario is one that I have encountered many times in my coaching, and the lessons learned here can apply to all coaching situations. It is about coaching someone who is close to you, and how you can keep "Tee for Two" from becoming "Divorce on the Course."

B. "COUPLES" COACHING

Golf is a wonderful game to share with someone you care about. When couples decide to play golf together, they usually dream about the delightful hours they will share on the course and the closeness they can have from participating in a common activity—one that they hope to continue throughout their lives. Like all couples, they want to enhance their relationship. This is certainly possible, but unfortunately it doesn't happen often.

I have given many workshops on couples coaching, and in 80 to 90 percent of the situations the husband starts out as coach and the wife as student. This percentage is changing as more women take up the game, but let's take what I feel is currently a typical scenario.

In the honeymoon phase, so to speak, this situation usually works out fine. The husband will give the wife tips on her swing and she will accept them. Sometimes the tips work, sometimes they don't, but in the beginning that's okay. After a while, though, the student begins to realize that the person who is teaching her is not an expert, and she becomes less trusting of the advice he gives. Correspondingly, the coach begins to get frustrated that his coaching (the student's improvement) isn't going as well as he had hoped.

At this point the couple often find that it's hard to leave each other alone, and the scene begins to get emotionally charged. The touchiness of the situation then makes the husband less likely to give suggestions and the wife less likely to ask for them. This usually evolves into a type of détente, a shaky truce during which the two don't talk much. At this stage you often hear comments like "Don't say that!" from the wife, and "Well, you were lined up that way!" from the husband.

After another period of time, the husband finds that it's easier to play golf with the guys because he doesn't have to be coaching all the time. The wife decides she is more comfortable with the gals, where she's not constantly being coached. They're both a lot freer and happier when they're not playing together. I've seen many cases where playing golf together has not only failed to fulfill a couple's high hopes, but it has actually backfired. What can be done to make this scenario different—to make it work the way people want? As I said earlier, there are three ground rules. Follow them and I guarantee that the situation will improve.

1. *Coach only when asked.* This is of utmost importance. Never, never coach someone unless you are asked to. The goal in any instructional situation is not the coaching but the learning, and people do not learn unless they are ready and receptive. Coaching must be initiated by the student.

So how does a person request coaching? I recommend that people ask in the simplest, clearest way: "I would like to be coached." That's the way, and that's the only way. If the wife tops her drive, throws her hands in the air, and shouts, "What did I do wrong?" that is *not* an invitation for coaching. That's an exclamation. The husband, if he wants to, can ask for clarification—"Would you like to be coached?"—but the wife must clearly ask before coaching is allowed. If someone hits a bad shot and says, "Oh @#%$&#@!" the partner does *not* have to come to the rescue. The language to request coaching must be clear, and it must be agreed on beforehand.

2. *Coach only what you are asked to coach.* The agenda—

the area of coaching—is determined by the student. The coach must stick to that agenda, and he must do it in an objective way only.

Let's say the wife asks to be coached on the length of her backswing. The husband then will serve as an extra pair of eyes to help confirm the validity of what she experiences. She takes her swing and then says, "I felt that it went all the way to parallel at the top" (the student always speaks first). The husband then responds with something like "It was a foot short of parallel." That's good coaching. One person says what she was aware of, the other says what he saw. However, if on the next swing the husband says, "It went all the way to parallel, and you shifted your weight very well too," he's stepped out of bounds. In the Couples' Coaching workshops that we do, the husband would have to spend five minutes in the penalty box. He has made an interpretation, and that's against the rules.

It's very important to understand that the coach has *no* interpretive powers and is only a mirror to reflect reality. The process should be as follows: The student makes an action, the student says what she experienced, the coach responds with what he saw. That's all. When people step outside these bounds and make judgments and suggestions, things start to fall apart.

3. *Coach only for a specific amount of time.* The coach-student relationship is good for certain situations, but if it hangs on and spills over into the normal relationship it can be a real problem. Setting a time limit allows both people

to get back to their own golf games and their regular relationship. It removes the necessity for one person to ask the other to stop, which can often result in hurt feelings.

To make these rules work requires a firm commitment, one that may be hard to keep at times. I have much direct experience with this commitment, having often coached my own mate, Johanne. One time I remember noticing that her alignment on the tee was pointing her directly out of bounds. I knew she was likely to lose her ball and I really wanted to step in and spare her the upset. But I held my tongue. She swung, and when the inevitable happened, she quickly looked at me to ask why I hadn't helped her out. But she held her tongue. We smiled at each other. We had kept our commitment. As far as the score on that hole went, we lost the battle, but we definitely won the war. We often play together now, sometimes with coaching, sometimes without, and it's always a delight.

To sum up, the ideal coaching situation would begin with the student making this type of request: "I would like to be coached on my backswing for ten minutes." The student would then swing and describe what she experienced, and the coach would respond with what he saw—for ten minutes, after which they would go back to being husband and wife. It works.

AND ALSO WATCH OUT FOR . . .

There are two additional important issues to mention in connection with couples coaching. The first one concerns the dangerous "W" questions: *What did I do wrong?* and *Why did I do it?* By their very nature these questions beg for interpretation and can thus lead to trouble. In the case of most couples, these questions require that a person who clearly is not an expert give what amounts to an expert opinion—shaky at best. And it's not the giving of an opinion that creates the problem, it's the annoyance and resentment that often follow when things don't work out as planned and the diagnosis seems to be the wrong one. Just remember that if you invoke the "W" questions, you will get what you ask for, but it may not be what you want.

The second issue concerns nonverbal, or "sneaky," coaching. Because usually couples know each other so well, they can engage in a form of coaching that has meaning to them but is undetectable to anyone else. I know a couple that is the perfect example. As the wife prepares to tee off, the husband will casually sidle up until he is directly behind her. As soon as he gets there, she'll say, "Move away, move away!" This happened once when I was playing with them, and I was perplexed. "Why do you want him to move?" I asked. "He's just standing there." The wife replied, "I know he's checking my alignment. He's always coming up behind me, and he'll tell me later on that I was lined up a certain way." This type of behavior comes under the heading "Mental Cruelty." It is definitely out of bounds since the husband was engaging in a form of coaching without being asked.

It is very valuable for couples to get in touch with these types of gestures, body language, and phrases—the ones that seem so innocuous but communicate so much. Exposing these subtle tendencies will help avoid the anger and resentment that often result from coaching.

THE BRIGHT SIDE

I said earlier that poor coaching technique can often cause a couple's efforts to backfire and make their golf less enjoyable than it was before. The opposite can also be true. Good coaching habits can spill over, and make not only golf but other joint activities more enjoyable. The principles outlined here can apply to any situation where one partner is learning from the other.

It is important to remember that the success of the coaching situation does not determine the quality of your relationship. The flight of the golf ball is not a barometer of your affection for each other—it's just a ball, and it goes where it goes. Don't forget what's really important.

The main reason that couples want to play golf together is so they can enjoy the game together. As Sam sang to Bogie, you must remember this: Always make sure that the fundamental things apply. It's easy to get sidetracked by your scores and all the social activities—Scotch Foursomes, Blind Bogey tournaments, etc. These can be a fun part of the game, but they are not essential. Here's something you might try to get back to basics. Go out to the course one warm evening, just the two of you, with only two clubs—a seven-iron and a putter—and play three or four holes. Maybe even do something crazy like play barefoot. Maybe even take a bottle of wine along. Forget about score, just go out and enjoy the sunset. Play golf as it was meant to be played—for the joy of the game—and play it that way together.

C. PARENT-CHILD COACHING

When a parent coaches a child, all the above guidelines apply. The parent-child relationship has much of the same intensity and potential problem areas as the couple's relationship. In fact, some areas of the parent-child coaching situation require even more vigilance.

As all parents know, a lot of the interaction with a child involves some form of teaching or correcting: "Sit up straight and eat your broccoli," "Please put your toys away," "Look both ways before you cross the street." Even though the parent has the child's best interests at heart, the volume and frequency of these directions can be overwhelming to a kid. It's very easy to continue this trend when coaching your child in golf, so it's important to make sure you observe rule #1: Coach only when asked. Certain adjustments may need to be made in the case of a very young child, but as much as possible, the goal should always be to let the child control the learning process.

Toward the beginning of the book I talked about my early golf years and how my father didn't coach me too much. This light touch gave me the freedom to experiment and develop a feel for the game, a sense I might never have gotten had I started out following too many rules. Of course a child may need some basic intruction, but make sure it's truly basic. ("Keep your head still," for example, is not what I consider a basic instruction.) Give your child room to explore and "play" golf, and I'm sure, as happens in most things, the child will amaze you with what he or she learns.

The coach-as-mirror process has particular advantages in the parent-child situation. Since the essential act of observation can be performed by almost anyone, the child can be a coach as well as a student, and a very helpful coach at that. In a parent-child coaching clinic that I recently gave, one family's goal was to have the seven-year-old daughter coach her father, who was a two-handicapper. This seemed impossible to most people, but unclouded by judgments and preconceived ideas of a correct swing, the child's perception was even sharper and more helpful than those of the experienced golfers in the group.

It can be a wonderful thing to let your child really help you with your game. In addition to giving him or her a strong sense of belonging and self-worth, this sharing of roles will most likely increase the child's receptiveness to being coached by you. It can change the dynamic of your golfing relationship, turning what was a hierarchy—you tell the child what to do—into a partnership in which you help each other. This shift can make a big difference in the quality of your relationship, not just in golf but in other aspects of your life as well.

SAFE AT HOME

Applying the three rules of coaching is only one part of creating a positive golfing experience for your child. An equally important aspect is the golfing atmosphere in the family—the point of view from which the game is seen. I feel it is vital for children to have a safe place where they can discuss their complete experience of the game, a place where they are not judged—and consequently don't judge themselves—by their score. They will get judgments enough from the outside world.

A good way to cultivate this type of atmosphere is to choose carefully the questions you ask your child when he or she comes home after playing. The first question should not be "What did you shoot?" but rather "What did you learn?" Now, this query may seem unusual to a kid, and since it can be hard to get kids to talk about themselves, you might get a response like "Huh?" or "I don't know." But I urge you to stay with it. It will force the child to pay attention to this important aspect of the golfing experience.

The second question you ask should be "Did you have a

good time?" Again, the replies you get at first may be minimal, but asking these questions lets the child know what your priorities are—what aspects of the game you feel are most important. As for questions about score, I believe families should not ask these. If the child wants to tell you, that's great, but otherwise let it go. You don't need to increase the child's awareness of score or incentive to score well. The rest of the world will take care of that only too well.

But in the final analysis, the best way for you to teach your child—and you've heard this before—is by example. Children learn most by who you are and what you do, not by what you say. If you want to make a difference in your child's golf game, make a difference in your own. As Tim Gallwey aptly puts it: You can't give away what you don't have.

If you want your child to view the game a certain way and be a certain kind of person on the course, work on being that kind of person yourself. If you want your child to play courageously, play that way yourself. If you want your child to keep his or her chin up when things aren't going well, keep yours up. If you tell your child to enjoy the game and be a friendly, supportive playing partner, but you become grumpy and reticent yourself when you're not playing well, which lesson do you think will have the most effect? Be the kind of person that you want your child to be, and that person will show up in your child. The point here is the same as throughout this book: It's who you are that makes the difference.

Chapter Seven

FEAR, COURAGE,
AND TRUST

Earlier in this book I talked about a round of golf I played at the California State Amateur Championship at Cypress Point. Just before the round began, I asked myself three specific questions, and after I had answered them I made a commitment to myself to play a full round of golf without fear. That was one of the first times I was conscious of the fear that had been so much a part of my game for so long. It was also one of the first times I mustered enough courage to confront it.

I honored my commitment, and what resulted was an extraordinary day. The happy ending to this tale would be that I conquered fear that very day and have played without it ever since. But this isn't the movies, and it didn't work out quite that way. Fear is still a part of my golf game, and my life. But the experience of that round gave me a much greater understanding of how fear affects my life, and I have since learned how to deal with it. I will explain by revisiting that round.

TOO YOUNG TO DIE

The commitment I made on that first tee gave me a new and extraordinary point of view. Examining the fear in my golf game made me aware of the role that fear had played in my life. I was only twenty-five years old then, but I had already begun to narrow the scope of my life. Because of fear, I had stopped pursuing activities that were too challenging, or that made me uncomfortable. I had begun to avoid anything—other sports, dancing, public speaking, even communicating honestly with others—in which I didn't have confidence, anything that was risky. I realized that my world was shrinking, and it shocked me.

At that point I had played in more than 150 golf tournaments, all over the country. For the first time, winning the tournament was not the most important thing. Dealing with fear was. I used to think that fear was a good thing, that it would protect me from danger and teach me what I could and couldn't do. But I began to see what fear was really doing to my life—it was killing me. I was only twenty-five, but in a way my world was closing down, and I was slowly dying. I realized that I was becoming the type of person I had always joked about: the analyzer, the worrier, the talker—not the doer. And I didn't like it. I had always read that fear in human beings was a valuable survival instinct, but I looked around and saw that I was not in a jungle and nothing was really threatening me. I could not see any way that my fear was helpful in my world.

That round of golf led me to explore fear and its effect

on people's lives. I became interested in the nature of fear itself—not just what I feared, but how I feared. With this new point of view, insights came from everywhere. Once during a golf lesson I was describing the sensations of fear—increased heartbeat, sweaty palms, tightness in the stomach. My student smiled and said that those were the same sensations he had had at his senior prom when his date whispered to him, "Let's go park somewhere." My fear and his excitement produced the same sensations, but our interpretations of those sensations were quite different!

It became clear to me that fear is not a set of physical sensations but rather the interpretation that we make of those sensations. And I realized that if we ourselves are the ones making that interpretation, then we must also have the power to make a different one. So when we feel these sensations, why do we consistently interpret them as undesirable and to be avoided? The answer, I feel, comes mostly from our culture. We live in a society in which the pursuit of comfort—and the avoidance of discomfort—is deemed a most valuable goal. But is comfort really what we want? One of the most meaningful things that my mother ever said to me was "I don't want to be comfortable, I want to be fully alive." And she was seventy years old when she said that.

Comfort and complete aliveness don't always go together. Learning and growth require a willingness to explore and take risks, which often leads to an initial feeling of discomfort and confusion. We are conditioned to label feelings of discomfort as undesirable, yet the best things in life always make us feel somewhat uncomfortable at first. Think about your own life. A new relationship, a new job, a new child—completely comfortable at the beginning? Of course not. By labeling these sensations as fearful and undesirable, we begin to narrow our lives. Fear limits our possibilities. The Art of the Possible consists of recognizing fear and not being stopped by it.

It has been twenty years since I chose to commit to courage during that round at Cypress Point, a commitment I still maintain today. I'd like to give you some conclusions I've come to since then. The first is that in all non–life-threatening situations in my life—and golf is certainly one—fear has never done me any good. Fear has not given me safety or learning; my intelligence has done that. Fear has not protected me from danger, it *is* the danger. Fear is simply a subjective interpretation, and I always have the power to make a different interpretation. I know now that the sensations and thoughts I once labeled as fear actually mean that I am getting close to an important discovery, and that I should keep going. Franklin Roosevelt said it best: "The only thing we have to fear is fear itself."

He must have played golf to get such an insight.

TRUST

Fear shuts down your life. It will not even allow you to attempt things. If you can see fear for what it is and keep going despite it, you can begin the learning process.

Courage will get you past the fear, but courage itself is not enough to keep the fear from coming back. Unless what you are doing becomes absolutely trustworthy, there will always be the potential for doubt and fear to recur. So let's see how you can develop trust in your golf swing.

Our daily lives are filled with complex and challenging actions that we do without even thinking twice. Driving a car, riding a bicycle, catching a ball—even running and walking—are really quite remarkable skills when you think about all the movements and subtle judgments they involve. Yet we do them continually, almost effortlessly, and with great confidence. Is hitting a stationary golf ball that much more difficult, such that people can practice it for forty years and still not be confident in their ability to do it? I don't think so. So the question remains: Why don't we trust our golf swing?

Let's begin this discussion by imagining the following scenario: You are walking down a hill. You catch your foot on a rock, stumble, and fall. You are left lying on the ground with a sore leg. The question is, Are you now afraid of walking? The answer is, No, you're not. Because you felt how your foot hit the rock, how you lost your balance, and how you fell, you would not now fear walking. You would be annoyed, certainly, but not afraid, since you were able to sense everything that happened.

Let's take another scenario. Suppose you're walking down the same hill and the next thing you know you're on the ground with your leg hurting. The result is the same as in the first scene, but this time you have no idea how you got there. Do you think you'd be afraid of walking now? Yes, you would. You would probably start walking the same way that most people play golf: tentatively, always looking for "something wrong." Why? Because you could not sense what was going on, and therefore you cannot be sure it won't happen again.

The ability to experience—to be aware and to feel—is what creates trust. If something is only in your head and not in your body, you don't own it and you can't really trust it. We know how to walk because we feel how to do it. We don't need to continually analyze our walking technique and we don't second-guess ourselves before taking a stroll. If we happen to stumble, we don't immediately go to the "walking range" for a practice session—we see it as just a stumble and trust that our walking abilities are basically sound.

The only way you can really trust your swing is if you can sense what is happening with it. The only way to develop this sense is to swing with a speed and a force that you can be aware of—never swinging faster or harder than you can feel. Once you swing and you have no idea what's going on, the words arise in your head that say golf is difficult.

You could take tap dancing lessons for years and years. You could read every tap dancing book and see every film on it. But if I injected Novocain in your feet you could never tap-dance. It ain't real if ya ain't got the feel.

OPENINGS

Being able to sense things as they happen is the basis for trust. Once you sense the distinction between balance and imbalance you can ride a bike, and you never forget how to do it. So how do you build that kind of trust in golf? When you start working on your swing, when you try to fix it, you actually stop feeling what's going on. By letting it alone you can sense it, in its original state. When you can do that, trust begins to grow.

When my students mention that I play better golf—closer to my potential—than they do, I ask them to tell me why. They say it's because I learned when I was young, I've spent more time on the game, I have more talent. These are just shallow explanations, not the real reasons why I play as I do. And they are dispiriting to students because they allow them no real openings or possibilities for improvement.

There is only one reason why I play better golf than most of the people I coach, and if you can get this, you will make tremendous progress in learning how to practice and how to build trust. I play better golf than most people because I am aware of things that they are not aware of, and I feel things that they don't feel. I sense distinctions in the full swing, in chipping, and in putting that they don't. These distinctions could exist for them, but they stay asleep while they swing and they don't experience what I do. Remember the walking scenario? I sense how I make my mistakes, what makes the ball go left or right, what makes it go long or short, what makes a solid hit. These distinctions are what build trust. You will never really trust your swing if you can't feel it. That which is trustworthy shows up in its entirety, without any major blind spots.

Think of the opening this gives you! It's not because I have more skill that I play better, but because I am more aware. Imagine going to the practice range with the idea that "I will improve if I become more aware of feelings and distinctions than when I started." Practicing becomes very simple. The object isn't so much to hit good shots but to really sense what's going on; the club going up, dropping and turning, moving through impact, following through. And you can start to become aware of your swing only when you stop fixing it. As long as you're thinking about what to do, it's very difficult to sense what's there. Awareness comes in the absence of trying to do things.

So wake up! It's a full-time job to stay asleep. Most people do it throughout their golf lives. They never sense what's happening in their golf swings, so they continually mis-hit certain shots, look at others and say, "What did I do? Did I lift up? Was my left arm bent? Did I come too far outside?" They are often confused, frustrated, and as I said in an earlier chapter, quite blind. Trust comes from feeling things in their entirety, and then believing in the reliability of what you have felt. Once you experience this, and realize how good it feels, you will have a strong motivation to keep at it. You will also begin to feel the difference between when you trust your swing and when you don't. Becoming aware of these differences—these distinctions—is what learning is all about. Swinging with confidence and trust is a whole new and wonderful way to play the game, and once you start there's no stopping you. Trust me.

No, trust yourself.

Chapter Eight

COMPETITION

Is there anything that has a greater effect on the way we live than our sense of competition? The way we look at competition—our basic survival instinct—has a profound impact not only on the way we play games but also on our relationships, our jobs, our views of society, our political decisions, just about everything we do. Recently, much has been said about the shift from the old, "jungle" way of looking at competition—the win-lose paradigm—to the more ecological, cooperative view—the win-win paradigm—and the positive effects this could have on all of us. Can golf give us insights into our sense of competition, and can these insights be valuable in other areas of our lives? Yes and yes, most emphatically.

To begin this chapter I would like to revisit my round of golf with the Ghanaian named Kojo, a match that I described briefly at the beginning of the book. What went on inside me during that round illustrates perfectly my approach at that time to competition. The realization of the effect this approach had on my game was the beginning of a profound change in my life.

DIFFERENT STROKES

I had expected to play a simple round of golf that day, but when I arrived at the course on my motorcycle I saw a fairly large crowd. As I mentioned earlier, I found out that the match had been billed as the Ghanaian champ versus the American champ, and I got a big kick out of that billing. Kojo was barefoot, wore a T-shirt, and had a very outdated set of clubs. I could tell immediately from his swing that I had had far more training and experience as a golfer. As I began the match, I was just enjoying being there, wanting to be a good Peace Corps ambassador and to have a close, exciting match, and hoping that I might be able to come back later on.

The first hole was a par 3, and I hit a five-iron to the edge of the green. Even though I hadn't played in a few months, I felt comfortable and my swing was the same as always. Kojo then took out his iron—I'm not sure which one it was—and hit a low scooter that landed about 100 yards out and bounced the other seventy up near the green. I turned to him and said earnestly, "Nice shot!" I had an attitude of openness and appreciation of both him and the situation.

I won a couple of holes at the beginning. I was outdriving him by thirty to fifty yards, I was relaxed and comfortable, and everyone seemed to be enjoying themselves. I was two up after eight holes.

On the next hole something happened that had a profound effect on my golfing life. Kojo won a hole. And as far as I could tell, he didn't change. He didn't seem to get pumped up or act any differently to me or the crowd. As we walked past the clubhouse to the back nine, he seemed to be having a great time just as before. But for me, everything changed. I began to create a scenario in my mind: "What would it be like if an experienced golfer got beaten by a barefoot amateur? What would people think of me? What would my friends say? Think of the embarrassment!" Now, for the first time, I abandoned my original goal of enjoying the experience. My goal became "Beat this guy."

I began to behave as most competitors: more distant, more separate from the situation. I continued to tell Kojo "Nice shot" at times, but my heart wasn't really in it anymore. I wasn't appreciating the skill and enthusiasm that he was displaying, I just wanted to win.

Kojo won the 11th hole and the match went to even. Now I *really* wanted to beat him, and I racked my brains for something I could do, some skill I might have to give me an advantage. On the 16th hole, Kojo won again and was one up with two holes to play. Now all I could think was "I hope he screws up." I began to focus more on his possible failure than on my own game.

On the 17th I again outdrove him by fifty yards. His approach was another scooter that bounced and bounced and bounced onto the front of the green. I said, "Nice shot," but it bore no resemblance to the compliment I'd given on the first hole. I hit my shot fifteen feet from the hole; his was ten feet away. My caddie took the mat that lay beside each "green" and smoothed the rough dirt between my ball and the hole. I desperately wanted to make the putt, but I wasn't really thinking about it. My mind was filled with two scenarios: what would happen if I made it, and what would happen if I didn't. And I didn't. Kojo stepped up to his ball the same way he always had and knocked it in.

The crowd surged in and picked up Kojo. They weren't disrespectful to me in any way, they were simply filled with joy. They carried Kojo all the way back home to his nearby village. I was left with my caddie and my feelings. I took no solace in the fact that I could probably beat Kojo four out of five times, or maybe even nine out of ten. What had happened was that I had screwed up my own performance, as I had for a good part of my life, but in the presence of someone who had not screwed up his. It was a significant moment for me.

As I mentioned previously, I realized then that even though Kojo and I were both playing golf, we were playing very different games. The pressure of competition—pressure that I had largely put on myself—was like a spotlight illuminating the differences between these two games. I realized that the way I was playing the game wasn't working very well and something needed to change. This change would directly affect my attitude toward competition. In the years since then I've come to understand what this new sense of competition is all about.

The Play's the Thing

Whenever we play golf or any other game, we do it for a reason—we hope to get some benefits out of it. People who compete well and don't get in their own way understand that the benefits of competition happen only during the event. These people seem to play very close to their potential and rarely tighten up. On the other hand, people who think that the benefits of an event come only when it is over will tighten up often.

If you feel that the joy and satisfaction of competition can happen only when the game is over—the praise and status that you get if you win—I believe that you will always feel a tremendous amount of pressure and have a hard time playing up to your ability. As much as you try, you can't control whether you win or lose. By making the success or failure of the situation dependent on something that is out of your control, you put yourself in a very vulnerable and pressure-filled situation. Your success, your status, and your self-esteem now hinge on the actions of the golf ball, which we all know can be very unpredictable. A foot to the left and you're a hero, a success, a "somebody"; a foot to the right (out of bounds) and you're a failure. Anyone will perform poorly when viewing the situation this way.

As discussed in an earlier chapter, a golfer's experience consists of a triangle of performance, learning, and enjoyment. If these elements are in balance, they all work well. But if they are out of balance, each one suffers. During competition most people focus on the result of their performance and ignore the enjoyment and learning aspects. When the performance begins to diminish, as it often does, they tend to intensify their focus, increasing the imbalance and making conditions even worse.

Learning and enjoyment come about during the event itself—they are not dependent on what happens after, and they are much more under your control than performance. The secret to competing successfully is being aware that the games of learning and enjoyment are under your control and winning them will give you the best chance of winning the scoring game, since it will ensure your best performance.

STAYING WITH YOUR GOALS

Over the years I have observed that many of my students understand, at least intellectually, this point of view and will begin competition with the overall game in mind. I find this very encouraging. However, as my round with Kojo demonstrated, the stresses of competition can easily change their initial, broad goals into narrow, performance-oriented ones. I emphasize this point with students in the following way.

At a point in the course walk I'll ask people if they prefer easy or difficult golf courses. Almost everyone answers that they like a course that's challenging. When I ask why, the common response is that it will help them grow and develop their game, indicating that improvement—learning—is a primary reason why they play golf. Then I'll walk up to a sand trap, drop in a ball, and step on it. I ask what everyone's typical reaction would be when faced with such a shot.

The consensus is that they would get upset and then call someone over to sympathize with the lousy lie. I pointed out that it seemed what they really wanted was to make sure everyone knew they had a tough lie, so that if they couldn't blast it out, at least no one would think they just flubbed the shot. They wanted to make sure not to look bad. This may be an understandable reaction, but nevertheless it is a clear case of switching goals. They started out wanting a challenge, but when actually faced with one, they forgot their original goal and reverted to the old standby of "looking good." Staying with your original goal is crucial for good competition, and like most other worthwhile endeavors it requires commitment.

The default commitment that usually predominates is the desire for others' approval, the desire to "look good." Winning the scoring game is often regarded as the ultimate way to look good, the focal point of this hidden commitment. But is this aspect of winning really worth all that focus? What benefits does this type of winning have?

Unless you are a touring professional (or a professional gambler), winning won't get you a significant amount of money. The praise and status you may get from winning can certainly be nice for a while, but as I discussed in the chapter on purpose, this attention doesn't last very long. In reality, winning the scoring game has very little lasting value. What do have real value, though, are the qualities you can develop and the type of person you can become through competition.

BLUEPRINT FOR CHANGE

Consider this possibility, for transforming your approach to competition. First, bring your commitments to light and find out what's really going on with you. If you are happy with your current priorities and way of competing, that's great. If not, there are plenty of other possibilities for you. Second, determine what benefits you would like to get from competition and decide what commitments you need to make to get those benefits.

This is the process that began for me when I lost that round to Kojo. I started with the idea of changing who I was by changing my commitments, and maintaining this focus was key to making the process successful. Over the years many different benefits and corresponding commitments have formed my goals, and maybe some of these are right for you. One of my first goals was being a courageous competitor—facing my fears—as I described in the trust chapter. Another was being a competitor who could handle upsets—like going from birdie to double bogey—with calmness and maturity. Yet another was believing in my abilities and letting go. These benefits are all connected, but at any one time there is always one that is uppermost in my mind. My current goal in competition is to keep an open heart.

We all know how winning tends to be portrayed in our society, particularly in televised sports, and it's not all that pretty. Winning becomes everything and the only thing; the victors are glorified and the losers humiliated. People who believe that by winning they elevate themselves and diminish their opponents are committing themselves to a lifetime of stress and pressure in competition. In my opinion, people who harden their hearts to their opponents and have little appreciation and compassion have already lost. My goal is to become a person who does not evaluate others (or myself) by a score, a person who competes with his heart wide open and with a joyful spirit. I know that if I can achieve this goal I will have already won, no matter how the scoring results may turn out.

THE REAL CONTEST

I believe that the true value of competition lies in the growth that it inspires in the competitor. The scoring game is not the end but the means by which this end can be achieved. The real contest is not you versus another but you versus you—your old self becoming a new self, and the struggle that this type of change brings. Your opponent is instrumental in inciting this growth, and the better the opponent—the closer the competition—the more benefits can result. Seeing competition in this way means a fundamental shift in perception. You begin to regard your opponent as your ally rather than your adversary. Strange as it may seem, you actually want your opponent to do well, in so far as it will make the competition as spirited and as close as possible.

This point of view completely changes the competitive landscape, turning a stressful situation with potentially humiliating consequences into a desirable situation with potentially great benefits. It's the difference between night and day, and it's obvious how this change could positively affect other aspects of your life.

BUSINESS AND BEYOND

Attitudes toward competition figure prominently in the many golf/business workshops that I give. As I'm sure you know, there is a powerful new trend in business thinking based on the concept of win-win negotiations—similar in spirit to what I have outlined above—in which both sides attempt to see each other not as adversaries but as allies working for mutual benefit. This is a very positive and hopeful trend, but as I said, it's a major change from the old way of thinking. It's really a change in culture, much as I described earlier when I talked about the Culture of Golfers, and so takes time and training to assimilate.

I have found that most people understand and support the win-win concept, at least intellectually. But applying it to their lives is another thing because let's face it, it's nice for the other guy to win, but we all want to make sure that we win too. So how do we know that it really works? It could be pretty risky if it doesn't work, so how do we test it out before applying it to our business and our relationships?

Golf is an ideal training laboratory. It provides an enjoyable, low-risk environment in which pertinent issues can be addressed and explored. Through golf it's easy to become aware of your approach to competition and try out new points of view. How do these new attitudes feel? Do they work? Do they give you more benefits? Do they allow you to win even more?

My experience as a golfer and a teacher makes my answers to all these questions a resounding "yes." The possibility that the game of golf can give people experience in such important areas, experience that they can apply positively in the rest of their lives, is truly inspiring to me. As I said at the beginning of this chapter, what has a greater effect on the way we live than our sense of competition? I am committed to helping golfers see there is another, more beneficial point of view.

CONSIDERATIONS

As in all aspects of the game of golf, there are many reasons why we compete. Most golfers, however, are limited to a narrow range of options, those concerned with winning and looking good. Consider the possibility of using competition to become a person of great character, full of integrity, open-hearted, and joyful. Consider making your motivation "What kind of person can I become through entering in this competition?" instead of "It's important that I win." Consider the point of view of who you are, not the point of view of what you want. Experience tells me that if you run your life by what you want, you will always feel a lot of pressure and anxiety. But if you run your life by who you are—a person of character—and accept what that gives you, I believe that you will feel much joy and will experience much growth during competition. And you will look forward to competition because it gives you great opportunity to learn not only about your golf game, but also about the person you are.

Chapter Nine

GOLF FROM THE FUTURE

Extraordinary people live their lives backward. They create a future, and then they live into it. Let me explain.

Most people believe that what they do now and what they will do in the future are based on what they have done in the past. They believe that their previous training, accomplishments, and behavior patterns are instrumental in determining their future patterns and accomplishments. This way of thinking certainly applies to golf: If we're playing poorly, we're afraid of being stuck in a bad streak; if we're playing well, we feel we're on a roll. If we have a bad practice, we become anxious about the upcoming round; if we practice well, we have high hopes. Seeing the past as the foundation for the present and future seems so obvious and so logical you may wonder why I even bother to mention it at all. Of *course* what we've done shapes what we will do—what else possibly could? Well, let's see what else is possible.

It has been my experience that people who play an extraordinary golf game and who improve extraordinarily live their lives in the opposite way. I believe it's possible that most people seek improvement in an entirely wrong dimension. We all look for a variation of what we already have. I am absolutely sure that our past has very little to do with how we play golf on any given day. I feel it's possible that golf is given to us not by our past but by our future. I know this sounds crazy, so let me see if I can clarify things by means of a story.

THE COURAGE TO CREATE

A few years ago I played a round at a course in Santa Cruz, California, called Pasatiempo. This was the third of the three most significant rounds of golf in my life, after the round with Kojo in Africa and the round at Cypress Point in Monterey, where I first became aware of the role that fear had played in my golf game and my life. By this time I had become aware that my future, the one that I had created for myself and was living into, was full of the possibility that my golf could be magnificent. This future gave me a way of "being" on the golf course, and that was the point of view I held when I entered the pro shop that day in Santa Cruz.

The professional behind the desk happened to know who I was and wanted to watch me tee off. I said sure. I passed some students of mine on the putting green on the way to the first tee, and they also wanted to watch me play. I welcomed them as well. I was living in the possibility that

I could play magnificent golf. This wasn't positive think-ing, really, but rather the simple act of keeping that possi-bility open and alive. As I stood on the first tee, I had a choice: I could worry about how I looked in front of a pro-fessional and my students, and about the possibility of em-barrassing myself. Or I could look down that first fairway and see the possibility of adventure—the possibility that I could just let it go and really express myself. I chose the second option. I took my first swing and really belted one.

I walked down the fairway still living in that possibility. I was talking to and enjoying the people with me. It was a beautiful day. I got to my ball and prepared for an ap-proach shot. I took a five-iron and hooked the ball into a thick clump of trees to the left of the green. It was a poor shot, and I had a terrible lie.

At that moment, I normally would have hung my head and berated myself: "There's that same old pull hook again! Why can't I get rid of it?" I would have been upset and embarrassed. My old routine—my past—would have taken over the same way it always had. But for the first time in my life, I actually understood that if I could re-create the future—the possibility of magnificence—right there, right then, it would be the most courageous act I could do in the game of golf. I realized that after I hit a poor shot I could go into my usual routine of worry and upset, or I could say to myself, "It *is* possible that I could play extraordinary golf starting right here."

All of a sudden things clicked, and it became an unbe-lievable day. I saw that re-creating a magnificent future was real courage. I walked into that clump of trees aware of the possibility that I could make a great recovery shot. And I did. Then I chipped it close and made my par. For once in my life I was able to leave my past in the past and not be bound by what it told me I could and should do. I created a new future for myself and lived into it all throughout that magical round.

LIVING IN THE LIGHT

Having a future that inspires you and gives you possibilities—that literally gives you life—has a tremendous impact on what you are doing at any moment. On that day in Santa Cruz, my new future didn't just change my actions or give me a few new choices, it completely altered my quality of life in that moment. I felt tremendously free, with a wonderful sense of unpredictability and adventure. The future I was living into altered the person I was being, and this change of being caused my actions to shift naturally and joyfully. It's almost as if I had said to myself, "Suppose I'm not bound to my past. What kind of a future would I like to create for myself?"

Creation means calling forth something from nothing. It has nothing to do with your circumstances. Extraordinary people are not bound by their circumstances; they are able to create their lives anew each day. Yet we all have this ability all the time.

I remember wondering to myself as I was playing that

day, "How is it that people's lives, which have such potential for being extraordinary, so often become ordinary?" Ordinary, I believe, simply means letting your past create your future, though most people don't realize that this is what usually happens. I know very few golfers who have a future that truly inspires them. They live and play with lots of hopes, but in truth expect the past to dictate what happens. They repeat the past over and over again.

In the course walk section at the opening of the book, I spoke about this flipping of the past into the future. I mentioned that the real reason people get upset over a bad shot is that they expect it to happen again. I used an example that bears repeating here: If you knew that you were going to flub your first shot but thereafter play the best round of your life, would you be upset after that first shot? You wouldn't, because you would know that you had a wonderful future ahead of you. But most of us are upset when we hit bad shots because we expect they will happen again. This means we don't really have a future that's open and full of possibilities but one that's already set in motion and has a pretty predictable outcome. People get upset in golf because they think that what happened in the past will continue to happen.

I spent some time when I was younger working for an organization called Suicide Prevention. Two nights a week I answered phones and talked to people who were in a bad way, people who believed that the future held no new possibilities for them. These people felt that the only future open to them was a repeat of their difficult and painful past. Now, I'm not saying that golfers are that extreme (although some of them seem like it at times). What I am saying is that having a predictable future is dispiriting.

There are tremendous numbers of people taking up golf nowadays, but there are also tremendous numbers quitting. I have read statistics stating that three out of four women who started playing golf in the last five years have quit the game. Why do these people quit? Most likely because they feel they have no future in the game. They feel that their past—with its frustration, embarrassment, and slow pace of learning—will continue.

What would it be like to create a future that enlivened and inspired you, and to be able to live into that future? When it comes to being extraordinary, it's not what you do that makes a significant difference, it's the person you are. And this sense of being is given to you by the future that you create.

THE OTHER SIDE

I know that the concept of your present being determined by your future is not very logical. In fact, most of the key ideas in this book appeal to the nonlogical part of our thinking—the intuitive, artistic, inspirational side. I believe this is necessary because of the imbalance in the way golf is currently taught and practiced, with far too much emphasis on logic and technique. But we can't ignore our rational mind, and I know that this part of your thinking will have a lot of questions about playing golf from the future.

These questions might be summed up as follows: "Maybe it's possible to create all kinds of wonderful futures for myself, but I can envision hitting 300-yard drives and shooting scratch golf all year long, and I don't think it's going to happen. All I'll do is get frustrated, and if I tell anyone about it I'll look foolish." What will make golf from the future different from the wishful fantasies and daydreams that we all have?

Well, there is a great difference between possibilities and expectations, and this book is about the former, not the latter. Now, it may seem like I'm dealing with semantics, but I'm really not. Expectations imply judgment, and they usually reduce the possible outcomes to two: the desired outcome (meets expectations), and the other, undesired ones (do not meet expectations). This is a clear win-lose situation, with all the accompanying anxiety and pressure.

Possibilities imply a free range of outcomes, any one of which could occur. There will certainly always be outcomes that are more desirable than others, but therein lies the Art of the Possible. Becoming aware of the vast range of possibilities, and then accepting with grace and maturity those that occur while still keeping open the full range, requires skill, courage, and a spirit of adventure. But it is indeed possible, and well worth it. Your very future depends on it!

There is a difference between possibilities and fantasies, and I think we all know what that difference is. Real possibilities inspire us to action, while fantasies tend to make us merely dreamers. If a future has real possibility, it pulls us toward it. If it is just a fantasy, it has no real connection with us. If a future truly enlivens and inspires us, then it is the right one.

RECAP

Extraordinary people live their lives backward. They stand in their future and determine how they would like their life to be. This vision of their future gives them a way to be in the present, and their actions spring naturally from this sense of who they are. Ordinary people simply live their past over and over again.

The first step to extraordinary golf is to create a future that inspires and enlivens you. But the real skill comes in re-creating this future in the face of the inevitable upsets that we encounter in golf. At any moment we have the choice of either letting the past continue—our usual routine—or living in the possibility of a new future. This Art of the Possible—distinguishing possibilities from expectations, accepting what happens with grace and maturity while keeping all possibilities open—is one of the most courageous and worthwhile things that a golfer can do.

INTERLUDE: THE JOYS OF CONVERSATION

"Hi! How's it goin'? How're you hittin' 'em?"

"Ah, you know, same old thing. I started out great. Had two birdies on the front, but on the back I missed a bunch of short putts. I swear some of 'em were in and jumped out. I make those and I have a pretty good round. How about you?"

"You know me, I keep hackin'. I've still got that slice but I played okay. Had a couple out of bounds . . ."

"How'd you do on number eight?"

"Oh, I made my weekly deposit into the lake. Hey, somebody's got to do it! Got a double."

"You ought to try this new driver I've got, with one of those new shafts. I bet you'd make it over the water with this one."

"Okay, what the heck. I'll try anything! Let's play sometime."

"Great. I think I have some time next week. I'll call you soon, all right? See you later."

"Good seeing you. Take care."

The golf conversation. The music of the links. Variations on this theme occur thousands of times every day on thousands of courses around the world. Whatever the country, whatever the language, the music is much the same, and we all know it well.

At its best, the typical golf conversation is an old friend—familiar, comfortable, and easy. Its recipe consists of a little success, a little more failure, some hope, some more frustration, and a dash of resignation, all wrapped up in the right amount of self-effacing humor. Sometimes it's exactly what you need, like the perfect after-dinner dessert. It can make you relax and smile like a favorite song on the radio. With its well-known rules and limitations, it can serve as a common language, an icebreaker just about anywhere you go. It can be an enjoyable and important part of the game.

Then again, it can be a real drag. The same old people talking about the same old things in the same old way. Who among us hasn't made the standard, polite overture—"How'd you do?"—and then had to endure, for what seemed like hours, a shot-by-shot description of a round? Who among us hasn't thought, "If I have to hear that guy talk about his slice one more time . . . !" How many times have we known exactly what the conversation would be before we even began it?

The social aspect of golf is one of the game's great joys. Being with old friends and making new ones is a big part of why we play. Conversation is the medium through which social interaction takes place. It not only reflects a person's experience of the game, but it helps to make that experience more real since, in a social sense, if you can't talk about something it doesn't exist. Some of the greatest benefits of a new approach to golf are the new possibilities for conversation.

CAN WE TALK—REALLY?

When I was in college I would often stay up late at night talking with friends. The reason I was able to keep such late hours was not just because I was young, but mostly because those conversations were so interesting and meaningful to me. Those conversations fascinated me, energized me, and changed me. I'm sure you know what I mean. We've all had those types of experiences, but unfortunately when we get older they seem to happen a lot less frequently. How many of those conversations have you had lately?

Society by its very nature fills our lives with rules and limitations, and these usually extend to our dialogue. We all know what kinds of conversation are appropriate for work, for PTA meetings, for parties, and so on. The conversations that I had in college would probably fall more in the spiritual realm of society (what is life all about?), although they concerned a lot more than spirituality. It seems to me that we all long for meaningful, energizing conversations, yet most people rarely have the opportunity to engage in them.

It often takes an extraordinary event, such as birth or

death, to break down social conventions and allow deep communication. When your child is born the world becomes a truly magical place, and your conversations at that time reflect that point of view. The tragic news that a friend has a terminal illness can allow you levels of conversation with that person you may never have had before. These are possibilities that always existed but that you may not have known you had. In such a case you may find yourself wondering, as many have, "Why didn't we talk like this before? Why did it take news like this to allow us to really communicate with each other?"

Conversations—those inside your own head as well as those with others—not only reflect your point of view, it may be said that they *are* your point of view. This book is about changing your point of view about the game of golf, so it is also about changing the conversations that you have in the game. When you open yourself up to a new way of looking at golf, you see a new world of possibilities that exist for your conversations as well as your game. And what a joy that can be.

The dialogue that I am able to have with my golf colleagues and students is as inspiring and energizing as any I have ever had. It enlivens my teaching and enriches my life. Even though I don't stay up late as often as I did in college (I am a bit older, after all), these conversations light me up as much as ever. When you talk about goals, commitments, fears, instincts, self-images, awareness—the content of this book—this tends to go a bit beyond your everyday golf conversation. But the fact that everything is seen in the context of golf—a game we all know can be absurd—keeps these conversations down to earth and grounded in a wonderfully human way.

Students at both the Golf in the Kingdom workshops and the School for Extraordinary Golf are continually amazed and delighted at the types of things they find themselves talking about—in a golf workshop, no less. And they are even more amazed by the fact that these conversations seem normal in this setting. Since this dialogue is deeper than what they are used to in golf, it is often accompanied by a greater variety of emotion than they are used to in golf. Yet the workshops are not encounter groups, and these emotions are rarely the kind that make people feel too uncomfortable or vulnerable. A game provides a safe context where people can have deep conversations and genuine emotions, yet not take them too seriously. This is a benefit that few students expect, but all students appreciate.

Does that mean that everything we talk about is profound and philosophical? That every dialogue reflects discussions on self-identity and the meaning of life? Of course not—who would want that? We engage in as much lighthearted golf banter as always and enjoy it just as much. The key difference is that we're not limited to it, and this makes all the difference in the world.

As I mentioned in an earlier chapter, having possibilities not only gives you more options for the future, it also transforms the quality of the present. Even if you rarely explore all your options, the fact that you have them profoundly changes your current experience. A good analogy might be the difference between a one-room apartment and a four-bedroom house. Although the single room of the apartment might be fairly large, it would still feel confining. But being in a similar room in the house would feel quite different, even if you spent most of your time in that room, since you would always know that you were free to move around. Possibilities make all the difference.

The point of view that most golfers have of the game, and their resulting golf conversations, are like the one-room apartment: functional but confining. As the real estate agents say, it's time for you to move up. And I've got just the listing: 4 BDRM, 2 BA, ON GLF CRSE, EXTRDNRY VU.

WHAT YOU SAY IS WHAT YOU GET

Your point of view, your conversations, and your experience are all part of the same thing. If you want to make and sustain breakthroughs in your view of golf and your performance, you need to make and sustain breakthroughs in your conversations as well. This is one of the biggest challenges that my students face, since what we're really talking about here is a new culture, one that is quite different from the existing Culture of Golfers. One comment that I hear quite often at the workshops is "I could never talk like this with the golfers at home—they just wouldn't get it." Maybe they wouldn't at first, but I think you'd find that it doesn't really matter.

We're all social beings—no man, or woman, is an island—and we're all very much affected by our social environment. It's a lot easier to be successful at something if our environment supports it. This support does not necessarily mean agreement, but it does mean awareness and acceptance of personal preference. For example, a person may not like the same movies that you do, but he or she can still accept your different tastes and thereby understand a little more about you. However, no one can support you in any meaningful way unless he or she knows what you're up to.

So here are my key points. To sustain breakthroughs you need the support of your environment—the people around you. In order for these people to support you, they must know what you're about, and you *must* make them aware of your new point of view—your new goals and commitments. If "who you are" when you play the game is really going to change, your social group needs to know who this new person is, otherwise they will continue to see you as they always have, and it will be harder for you to change.

Now, this isn't as risky as it might seem at first. Yes, there is a possibility that some people will think you're strange, and yes, it will take some courage, but nothing ventured, nothing gained. As I have said throughout this book, I'm not trying to show the right way and the wrong way to play golf, I'm simply trying to present new possibilities for the game. If you communicate your new goals and commitments in a straightforward, nonjudgmental way—"here are some ideas that I'd like to try out"—my experience tells me that they will be well received. From what I have seen, and I've been golfing a long time, the vast majority of golfers really want to be friendly and helpful, and all you need to do is give them the chance.

TEE TALK

Let me give an example of a typical situation and how it might be different. Let's say you're on the first tee at your home course and about to play with a couple of people you've never met. In this situation, what usually happens after the introductions is what might be called nervous small talk, and it tends to follow a familiar pattern. People might say things like "I haven't played for a few weeks so I'm a little rusty," or "I've been working on a new grip and it still feels a little strange," or "My back's been sore lately so I'm trying to swing a little easier." I think you know the tune. We're so used to this kind of talk that we usually don't think twice about it, but if we look a little deeper we can find out what's really going on, and it's very interesting.

Whether they are aware of it or not, most golfers are committed to looking good and not being embarrassed. Comments like the ones above naturally result from such a commitment. Here's what this talk really means: "I want to lower your expectations of me because if you have high expectations and I don't measure up to them, I'm afraid you won't think much of me, and then I'll feel bad." This point of view—that performance is most important, and if I don't perform well I'll look bad—gives rise to the conversations and the pressure that we often feel on the first tee and throughout the round. This is the normal way; this is the ordinary way. But it's not the only way.

Suppose that you said something like "You know, I've always been nervous on the first tee, and I'm working on trying to just swing freely and not worry about it. Wish me luck!" You simply let people know that you have your own particular focus. It's a different approach, certainly, but it's not all that odd. Rather than causing people to look at you strangely, I think you will find that this approach can create an opening that will lead to better conversations and a more enjoyable round.

We all have fears on the first tee. We are all eager for conversations that are more than the same old thing. We all would like to be friendly and supportive. Instead of the usual "Nice shot" when you hit a good one, or awkward silence when you don't, this new opening gives people another way in which to show support. Letting your basis of conversation depend on something other than performance can also be much more relaxing and enjoyable. You really can't control what the golf ball does or what your scores are. If you're in the "two shots from being crazy" mode, which many golfers are, those two shots can make dramatic and awkward changes in your conversations as well. However, a goal such as swinging freely is much more under your control and thus much less likely to turn sour. And I think you and your playing companions will find that it's more interesting as well.

CONVERSATIONAL ART

Creating and sustaining breakthroughs in conversations does not mean that you have to become unrecognizable to your friends. It's not so much changing who you are as becoming more of who you really are. The possibilities in perspective, performance, and conversation that I discuss have always been available to you. You have always had these possibilities, so you really haven't changed but have just become more aware. The way I see it, thinking, acting, and talking in these new ways is quite normal; it's the Culture of Golfers, with its narrow perspective, that seems really strange. Integrating these new ways of being into your normal conversations is another facet of the Art of the Possible, and it's not so difficult.

Let me give you a personal example. My father just turned eighty, and he's fortunate to be healthy enough to be an active golfer. He lives only a few hours from me, and we try to play golf together as often as possible. Sometimes we even take golfing vacations together, and we have gone to places such as Scotland and the Carolina coast. We hardly could have enjoyed these times together more.

My dad has seen me grow and develop over the years and is well aware of my work. We've had lots of conversations on all the ideas in this book. Yet when we're on the course we mostly talk like any other father-son pair: filling each other in on family members, asking about each other's health, checking in on finances ("You doing okay—anything you need?"), talking about upcoming plans, etc. And of course the typical golf stuff: laughing, moaning, cheering, groaning, whooping, whining—the stuff that makes it all so much fun. In a four-hour round we may only spend fifteen minutes talking about things that are beyond the usual range of golf conversations. It's not so much the time we spend—some days we may not talk like that at all—but it's the fact that we are able to do it whenever we want that's important. We don't have the barriers to conversation that most people have. The talk is free to go where we want—even to "profound" areas—and it goes there smoothly and easily. At first we were very aware when the talk shifted to new realms, but time continues to smooth out any rough spots, and now it seems completely normal. This freedom is truly a joy, and it greatly enhances our relationship.

The Art of the Possible is seeing possibilities and being able to move freely through them without getting stuck. You can experience this art directly in your conversations as you let your talk flow to whatever interests you the most. This is an extraordinary thing, but the real skill consists in making it normal. Making the extraordinary normal is what this book is about.

Chapter Ten

THE SOURCE OF CONSISTENCY

Almost all of my students over the years have said that they would like their golf games to be more consistent. According to the dictionary, "consistent" means conforming to a regular pattern or style—unchanging. What golfers mean when they talk about consistency, however, is somewhat different. Let me take a moment to find a working definition of consistency, then I'll talk about how it might be achieved.

Consistency in golf would seem to refer simply to consistent scoring—regularly shooting rounds that are within a few strokes of each other. Yet scores can be achieved in a variety of ways: in regulation (down the middle, on the green, and two putts), or by scrambling (in the woods, in the trap, then up and down). From my experience, most people are thinking about the first way when they talk about consistency, so our definition must include not only consistent scores but consistent shots as well. A consistent golfer, then, is one who shoots pretty much the same scores in pretty much the same way.

But of course nobody would really want to be like this,

even if the resulting score were a good one. Recently a friend of mine, Steve McGee, attained a level of consistency he had long dreamed about: He began to regularly shoot around 75 in much the same way each time. But what he thought would be a joy has now turned into a trap that he longs to escape. In his words: "I thought it would be golfing heaven, but it's golfing hell." No one wants to be stuck at the same level of play, no matter what that level is. We must expand our definition of consistency to include consistent improvement. The definition now reads: Fairly similar scores produced by fairly similar shots with fairly regular improvement. Let's translate this into real golf terms.

KEEPING THE GAME GOING

My brother and collaborator, Pete, was for many years the antithesis of a consistent golfer. His booming drive on one tee was often followed by one that would end up in the next fairway, or even two fairways over. Because he knew what kind of game he was playing and accepted the consequences, he was always fun to play with. Recently, however, he began to adjust his swing in order to play more consistently. He was frustrated at not being able to count on having a friendly competition with his regular playing partners. His scores were so erratic that it was very hard to determine how to handicap him. What he wanted was to play consistently enough to make sure that the "game"— his own golf game and the one he set up with his friends—

didn't fall apart. And I think, in a sense, this is what we all want.

Whether competition is involved or not, playing the game is what the game is all about, and we need to keep the game going in order to keep enjoying its pleasures and benefits. I think that the essence of what we want when we talk about consistency is the feeling that when we go to play golf, the person who shows up will be one we know and trust. And we want to feel that the person we are when we play is someone that we and our playing partners can rely on to be "in the game." It's hard to get a handle on someone who shoots 85 one day and 100 the next, especially with the mood swings that often accompany such variation. We know we can't play golf like a machine, always hitting the same shots in the same way, but neither do we want to blow up and embarrass ourselves. This dependability that we seek should ideally lead to feelings of satisfaction and fulfillment. This is my sense of what golfers mean when they say they desire consistency.

Most people have occasional periods of exceptional play, but in truly extraordinary golf these periods will occur more regularly. Consistency is a crucial element of extraordinary golf: the ability to stay on the path and to sustain the breakthroughs. As I see it, there are three increasingly deep levels of consistency.

LEVEL 1: AWARENESS

The first step on the road to consistency is awareness of the reality of your swing, and this awareness can begin only when you stop trying to fix your swing. Being in constant fix-it mode prevents you from being aware of what you are doing when you swing. It is impossible to achieve any stability or regularity if you are constantly trying to fix something and you don't even really know what that something is. The only consistency you will achieve is consistent frustration, something we've all had enough of.

An outside-in learning approach is inherently unstable. It is difficult, if not impossible, to achieve any measure of consistency when you are always looking outside yourself for the answers. You will be continually at the mercy of what's in fashion—the latest swing style, the latest magic golf club, the latest miracle cure—and what's in fashion is constantly changing. The only things that you can really depend on are those things that you do instinctively and naturally. As you become more aware of your swing, you become more in touch with these instincts. In its wonderful way, simple awareness begins to shape your golf swing more and more along your natural instincts. A golf swing based on these instincts will be dependable and consistent, and I believe that it is the only truly consistent swing that you can have.

Here is the progression:

1. **Not fixing your swing** allows for
2. **Awareness** of your swing, which allows you to

3. **Clean up the blind spots,** which permits a high level of
4. **Trust,** which allows for
5. **Letting go,** which is the basis of
6. **Consistency.**

This is the path to consistency; these are the breakthroughs that allow it to happen. I have gone through this process of focusing on awareness and not fixing it with many people. Typically, after a short period of time (anywhere from a day to a week), a person starts to settle down and play pretty good golf. The process starts to work, the person begins to have confidence in it, and progress is made. But by this time the person has left the supportive workshop atmosphere and is back in the normal world of golf. There is one overwhelming reality in this world, and the pull of its magnet is strong. In too many cases, I have seen the old habits of formulas, tips, and judgments undo much of the progress the person has made.

I am not interested in teaching a person to play pretty good golf for a short amount of time. I am interested in the possibility of sustaining a high level of progress and performance for as long as a person wants to play. I am confident that the path of awareness and instinct is the correct one, so the next step is to find ways to keep ourselves on it.

LEVEL 2: COMMITMENT

Once we have determined the path we want to be on, how do we stay on that path? Where do we find the sustenance, the focus, to keep us on course day after day? These questions, of course, are relevant to almost any field of endeavor, not just golf. Like many people, I have been looking for the answers to them all of my adult golfing life. Let me share my experience with you.

I used to think that I could find this steadiness by taming my mind. I thought that I could make it like a steel trap, and only what I wanted would enter. But after more than eighteen years of trying to do this, I have realized that it's never going to happen. Thoughts fly in and out like birds dropping bits of information (and other things too), and I don't have any real control over them. Even now, when I'm over a shot, a thought like "What would happen if I top it?" will still pop in. Over the years, I have learned to manage these thoughts a lot better by realizing I don't have to buy into what they say. Nevertheless, the same thoughts, the same internal conversations, are still there. I don't believe that the mind can be controlled, and thus it cannot be expected to demonstrate consistency.

I had also thought that I might be able to control my body in this way. I hoped that with enough of the right kind of training, my body would become dependable enough to produce the steadiness I sought. However, I think most people have a pretty good sense of the futility of this effort. It is natural for our bodies to change from day to day, and there is very little that we can do to control these changes. Our bodies are marvelous things, with amazing abilities, but like every other living thing on earth, they fluctuate. Training our bodies alone will not give us the consistency we seek.

My next area of hope was my attitude and emotions. I thought that enthusiasm and a positive, upbeat attitude might pave the way. Even though I am probably emotionally more steady than the average person, I am a long way from having any real consistency. I realize now that for me, not only is it impossible to control emotions, it's probably not healthy even to try. Consistency will not be found there.

So consistent growth, enjoyment, and fulfillment that could be called extraordinary will not, in my experience, come from consistency in your mind, your body, or your emotions. Extraordinary golf comes from another source, and that is commitment. What you are committed to is what makes the difference. Your commitment is your anchor, your taproot. It gets you out of bed in the morning and keeps you going in the right direction. It helps you withstand the pulls and distractions of the ordinary golfing world. Commitments are the foundation of consistent play.

A GOAL IN EACH SWING

At any moment, we are always committed to something. The first step in creating meaningful commitments is to become aware of our current commitments. Common hidden commitments, as I have said, are looking good, not being embarrassed, making sure we're right, and even, at times, dominating others. These are ordinary commitments and will produce nothing but ordinary results. Extraordinary golf requires extraordinary commitments, ones that you find are truly inspiring. The deeper and more exciting the commitment, the more likely it will be to keep you on your chosen path.

So what fires you up? What really gets you going? Freedom? Joy? Confidence? Courage? What were the qualities that characterized your best rounds, your most enjoyable days on the course? What kind of a person were you on those days? These are the areas in which to look for powerful commitments. We tend to focus on and remember results, but these are secondary. Look to the primary causes, the things that allowed the results to happen.

My experience with myself and other golfers has shown me that there are two very helpful guidelines in choosing effective commitments. The first is that the best commitments are those that can be realized in every swing. In other words, you should not require more than one swing to achieve your goal. A commitment such as swinging with freedom or courage can be achieved in a single swing. This type of commitment allows continuous feedback and frequent satisfaction, and is very much under your control. This combination makes it very powerful. A result-oriented goal, such as shooting a certain score, takes a long time to realize and is vulnerable to outside conditions. It is not nearly as strong.

The second guideline is that the most effective commitments are those that involve more than just you. Golf is often seen as a solitary activity, and although the primary interaction is between a golfer and him- or herself, some of the greatest joys of the game come through our interaction with others. If the commitment reflects this, so much the better. Let me give an example: If you make a commitment to work out regularly and get in shape, and your main reason is to look good, that may be enough to keep you going. But if you envision the new revitalized you as being a delight to your mate, an inspiration for others, a more cheerful and patient parent, and so forth, I think you will have a much better chance of success.

One thing that I have learned about achievement in golf is that it's a lot easier if you don't have to do it alone. So it is also crucial, as I said in an earlier chapter, that you make others aware of your commitments in order to allow them to support you. The combination of truly inspiring commitments and a supportive environment is a winner and will give you the best opportunity for consistency.

But there is still another, even deeper level. Commitments come from the intellect, and the head is the best way to begin. But we are much more than just our intellect—we have a heart as well.

LEVEL 3: THE HEART OF CONSISTENCY

Throughout this book I have said that extraordinary changes come not just from doing things differently but from a new way of being. Extraordinary is the result of a new point of view, which creates, in essence, a new person. The deepest level of consistency concerns the discovery of who you are. Now, the phrase "finding out who you are" is a delicate one. One moment it can seem like a solid philosophical concept, the next like a vague cliché best suited for a New Age comedy routine. But it's the best phrase to use here, and I know that most people have an intuitive sense of what I'm trying to say.

It is possible to perceive our lives as a continuous search for who we really are. We don't usually talk about it in this way, preferring to use phrases like "just trying to survive" or "pursuing happiness" or "looking for love," all of which are certainly appropriate. But the search for identity is paramount in everything we do. This is obvious by the way we use the identities that we have in society to describe ourselves. "Hi, I'm Fred. I'm a golf teacher." "My name's Lynn. I work for a health-care company." "That's Ron over there. He's a contractor. Plays to about a five handicap— hits the ball a long way."

Starting at a young age, we define ourselves by our activities and accomplishments. Yet as we grow and change, our activities change, and so also do our identities. Sometimes these can vary even from day to day. I remember being in high school and thinking, if I had a bad score on a test, "Maybe I'm not the best student, but I'm a good golfer." And if I had a bad day on the links, "I might not be the best golfer, but few people could be as good a student-athlete as I am." The process of determining who we are is very intense as we are growing up, and it continues throughout adulthood as well. It can become a full-time job, particularly since we tend to look for our identities outside ourselves.

In the same way that looking for the perfect golf swing outside ourselves is inconsistent and frustrating, so too is seeking an identity from the outside world, and these two things are connected in a meaningful way. Our identity is vitally important to us—it's our uniqueness, our individuality—and the quest for self-identity extends to games as well. Since most golfers look for an identity in the game and base it on how they swing and how they play, the golf swing and its results take on a great deal of significance.

Most golfers feel as if they have to prove themselves—define who they are—on every shot. This requires a tremendous amount of energy and attention, and it is the main reason why most people have difficulty developing real swing awareness. It can also lead to undesirable forms of identity. We all know golfers who see themselves as poor chippers, putters, or drivers. The quest for identity is so strong that it is very common for people not only to adopt a negative image but to hold onto it even in the face of contradictory evidence—a good putt is just an aberration because really I'm a lousy putter. They have their story and they stick to it.

Determining your commitments by things outside yourself, as I discussed in the second level of consistency, is just a reflection of this deeper level of determining your entire identity with regard to outside forces. Since our goal is to reverse this process and have our commitments come from the inside out, we must similarly reverse our search for identity. How do we do this? I have a sense of how it might be done, and I'll do my best to describe it to you.

DIFFERENT YET SO ALIKE

When we observe people, we primarily notice their differences—height, weight, hair color, age, looks, job, talent, wealth, marital status. We focus on the unique combination of characteristics that makes one person different from another. This is very natural and practical for our day-to-day living, yet often we focus on these differences to such an extent that they become all that we notice about a person. We forget about the vast number of things that we all have in common: trying to make a decent living, working to have a satisfying relationship with our mate, living with insecurities about finances and health, hoping to make a better world for ourselves and our children, looking for acceptance and approval from our friends and acquaintances, trying to be a better golfer. The list is endless, and it makes our differences seem small by comparison. After all, we are all human beings.

Consider the possibility of looking at people and focusing not on their differences but on their similarities. If you make this small but very significant change, you will feel the world change. You will come to realize that the things that make people different are the things that are most variable, and the things we all have in common are the most permanent, the most consistent. Herein lies the key to what I'm talking about: You will touch the heart of consistency when you begin to base your identity on the parts of yourself that do not change—the fundamental qualities that are common to all people.

Extraordinary comes from who you are, and if it is to be consistent, then who you are must be consistent. You are not really a manager, carpenter, therapist, student, runner, artist, low-handicapper, etc. This is what you *do*. Extraordinary is about moving beyond these mere concepts. This level of knowledge allows for the self-concepts to stop changing; it allows you to stop *thinking* of who you are and actually experience and express it—consistently. The question of who you are goes beyond your outside identity. It's a question about what doesn't change. The extraordinary that you look for in backswings and downswings, in your job and in your relationships, is not only inside you, it *is* you.

The three levels of consistency that I have described correspond to a familiar view of human beings, that we are made up of body, mind, and spirit. The physical actions of consistent golf must be connected to and supported by a consistency in mind and heart. Your thoughts, attitudes, and emotions may change when you hit a bad shot, but there is a part of you that doesn't change. This is the deepest part of you, and when you can experience it, and play golf from it, you will have tapped into the source of consistency. Your golf will no longer be a search for who you are, it will be an expression of who you are, and it will be filled with qualities of the heart: gratitude and appreciation.

Chapter Eleven

GOLF AS ART

art *n.,* 1. the production of something beautiful. 2. any practical skill, *the art of sailing.* 3. the conscious use of skill and creative imagination. [*To which I would like to add . . .*] 4. a contribution to others.

"**Y**es, but is it *art?*"

We've probably all seen this comment or something like it as a cartoon caption somewhere. Two serious-looking academic types pondering a bizarre painting or sculpture—it's been done in a lot of funny ways. The joke, in part, is that this question is far too broad and vague to result in any useful discussion or to have any practical applications. Is the question "Can golf be art?" worthwhile asking? Can it lead to new insights on how to play the game? I believe so, particularly if you ask a second question: "When does golf become art?"

The dictionary definition of art uses the art of sailing as an example. Now, I've never sailed before, and if I took out a boat I'm not sure the experience would be artistic. I would probably spend most of my time just trying to keep afloat and avoid being hit by the boom. But I feel that I play golf artistically, so what is it that makes the difference? An obvious answer is skill level: I am a much more skillful golfer than sailor, so my golf is artistic and my sailing isn't. There are many other possibile answers, however.

I believe that Golf as Art may have very little to do with skill level. I believe that anyone, beginner or pro, can play golf in an artistic way and have experiences so deep and compelling that they will benefit others as well. Let me begin my explanation with a short discussion about golf books that I have read.

A STORY OF STORIES

My house is filled with golf books—instructional, humorous, historical, inspirational, biographical, the whole gamut. I have read them all at least once, and some, such as *Golf in the Kingdom,* many times. I would like to talk for a moment about the historical and biographical books— those based on fact. Many of these books tell the story of a famous golfer or a famous match. They go into detail on a particular golfer's development, training methods, thinking processes, insights, etc. They often discuss historical trends in golf and important milestones such as the Vardon

Grip. They are typically well written and backed by impeccable research, and they are good stories. But in my opinion that's all they are—stories.

Now, I like a good story as much as anyone, and I'm willing to grant the author a reasonable amount of artistic license in producing one. But for me to accept that a book is based on reality, it has to feel somewhat real to me—it has to bear some resemblance to experiences I have had as a golfer. And over the years I've realized that few of these books really do.

We all know the elements of a good story—the hero, the plot, the challenges, the setbacks, the triumphs. There is an order and a flow to events and a certain logical progression, and the lessons learned from each experience build steadily. Even when you add disappointment and tragedy, there is a comfort, pleasantness, and familiarity to the whole thing, and that's how I think of these books.

Now, it's possible that the golfers who are the subjects of these books are very special people and have had lives very different from mine and those of my students. Their experiences may have really happened in this storybook form, but I doubt it. I have been around enough to be pretty sure that their experiences were much like mine, and mine have not been nearly so comfortable nor logical as the stories describe. My experiences are filled with a great deal of chaos and nonsense. Things did not happen smoothly or logically, and one lesson did not inevitably lead to the next. I have done much wandering, stopping and starting, bouncing around, and being confused. I'm not saying that it's been miserable—not at all. It's just been different than the typical story.

Real life and real golf don't happen like a book. They don't follow a standard formula: they simply happen. This isn't a problem if you just want to write a good story, but it can be a real problem if you're trying to get in touch with your own experiences. We hear so many stories, and the story form is so powerful and seductive that we expect our lives to be like one. We see our lives as an ongoing story with ourselves as the main character, and we expect the scenario to play itself out with the form and drama that we see in books and movies. This process can be so strong that we will often ignore experiences that don't fit the story line.

When we have an experience, we develop a belief about that experience. It's usually the belief that we are most aware of and that we communicate to others. This can occur also when we consider other people's experiences. I think this must be what happens with many golf writers. They have a preconceived idea of what the experience should be like, and soon the experience comes to be perceived that way. I have begun to realize that most people, in their golf and in their lives, will ignore large parts of their experience and believe only the story that they create for themselves.

We have beliefs about the way things ought to be, and these beliefs obscure our perception of how things really are. The first step in playing Golf as Art involves giving up these beliefs and experiencing what is really happening. Real experience contains a lot that doesn't follow a story line, a lot that seems random and chaotic. It's not necessarily unpleasant or undesirable, but it's usually seen that way because it doesn't fit the story. Trying to rid ourselves of the chaos only leads to denial of our experience, because the chaos will always be there. I believe we need to embrace the chaos and learn to dance with it. And in that dance lies art.

LEAP OF MUSIC, LEAP OF FAITH

There is a well-known pianist named Keith Jarrett who is a wonderful example of what I'm talking about. He is known not only for his compositions but for his brilliant improvised concerts—music that he creates on the spot in front of large crowds of people. As he tells it, he does not prepare for these concerts in the usual way. He does not listen to his music or practice specific pieces the day before. He does not think about what he is going to do. On the day of the concert, he simply walks out in front of a few thousand people, sits down at the piano, and starts playing.

He says that he starts out somewhat synthetically, with his memory and training leading the way. But there comes a point when the creative process really begins—a point where, as he calls it, he "jumps" into the music. When he "enters" the music, the concert really begins. This is the point, I believe, where art takes place.

Art happens in the absence of formulas and prescriptions. It happens when you become completely immersed in what you are doing. It happens when you and your stories about yourself disappear. What shows up is something new and unique, alive and extraordinary—a new possibility that is created right there, right then. This experience is so intense that it can encompass more than just one person. When Jarrett makes the leap, I believe that the audience leaps with him.

Golf as Art happens in the same way. You start out playing your usual round, but there can come a point—maybe as you're walking down the fairway, maybe in the pre-shot routine—where, if you're lucky, you can "enter" the game of golf. That is the time, I believe, when golf truly exists for people. You become totally immersed in the game, time seems to disappear as creativity begins, and what emerges is extraordinary golf.

At this point golf changes from a noun to a verb; action, rather than thoughts about action, controls the situation. Golf is not a thing that you enter, golf is *when* you enter. And until you do, I don't think that you really play golf. Until you do, you are removed from the game much like a spectator is removed from the action on the field. Only when you are able to get onto the field can you be creating the game.

Interestingly enough, Golf as Art does not always have to be great golf. The result of the shot and the score are not really significant. It's so much more the moment, and so much less the golf. If you are able to enter the game, I believe that the experience will be so vital both for you and for others that it will be a pivotal point in your life.

To be able to leap into the game you must be willing to give up your story, give up your formula—even, in a way, give up your identity—and this can be scary. Many people think that they have to improve before they can let go and leap, but it doesn't work that way. I've noticed that even very good players have a hard time doing it. Even they tend to hold back, to cling to a formula and remove themselves from their actual experience in order to monitor it and edit it to fit their story. But there is no such thing as a practice jump, no partial way to do it. In the moment of practice or play, you must simply go. It is much more important to leap—to enter the game and to be fully involved, fully connected—than it is to swing correctly. I love practicing golf, but it's the leaping that's the most important. And the only way to practice this is to do it.

MORE THAN YOU EXPECT

I think that in our society we've gotten to the point where just hitting a few good shots and having a good time is reward enough in a round of golf. For this four or five hours of our time—which over the years can become a significant portion of our lives—this is all we've come to expect. Now, there's nothing wrong with hitting some memorable shots and having a good time, but it's possible for the game to be much more than that. I know that at times it can be such a powerful and moving experience that you have need for silence and reflection when you finish. It's like the moment of quiet that comes when the curtain closes on a wonderful play and everyone in the audience realizes that they have been part of something very special. Certainly every round can't be like that, but it doesn't matter. The possibility is always there, and for me, that is enough.

When I'm on a golf course and I play like that, I know it affects everyone in my group. When I leap, everyone leaps, and we share an experience that is meaningful for all. I think many people have had this type of experience, although they might not have thought of it in this way. It may have occurred in a foursome or while watching a tournament. Many of us have been fortunate enough to witness, either in person or on television, professional golfers enter the game in this magical way. When it happens, everyone is aware of it—there is a presence about the golfer and a feeling in the air, and we all get swept away. It's what we hope for in competition, and it is immensely pleasurable. This feeling can even happen on the driving range. People have said that Ben Hogan could mesmerize an entire crowd, including other golf professionals, with his practice. But it wasn't Hogan that everyone was fascinated by, because Hogan, in a sense, wasn't there. It was golf—as art. Golf as a contribution to others.

In coaching my intention is to look for a point where I can join in the student's experience. A point of entry, where we can get past the thoughts and the stories and be fully present, creating as we go. When it happens, it is the most exciting, enjoyable, effective coaching that I can perform. Most people think they're not good enough to have these kinds of experiences in coaching or in playing, but I disagree. You don't have to shoot par to play Golf as Art.

JOIN THE CLUB

Golf is not about courses, equipment, handicaps, or techniques. Golf is what happens to you when you play. Yet most people seem to see the "real" game of golf as some kind of exclusive club to which only the best golfers belong. To get in you must know what they know, you must have what they have. So most people ignore the lessons of their own experience and focus their energy on the formulas that these good players give them. But these formulas, I strongly believe, are just other stories.

As you probably know, the great Bobby Jones made a series of instructional films in which he explains in great detail everything about his golf swing and playing philosophy. People purchase these tapes in hopes of learning to play the way Bobby Jones played. But is this really how he learned to play? In an interview given near the end of his life, Jones said, "The golf swing is too complex to be controlled objectively, by what you've consciously learned." When asked what he relied on when he swung, he replied, "Instincts. Instincts I honed after practice combined with playing. The more I depended on those instincts—the more I kept conscious control out of my mind—the more nearly the shot came off the way I visualized it."

Now, I never talked to Bobby Jones, but I feel strongly that he learned to play golf through experience, awareness, experimentation, and instinct—trying new things, rejecting them, coming back to them, making progress, falling back, feeling confident, feeling confused. I don't believe that he learned to play by following the system he describes in his tapes. But in order to make the instructional tapes he needed to describe his experiences—he needed to come up with a story—and he did. The result is sincere, honest, logical, and fascinating—it's a great story. But it's his belief about his experience, not his actual experience, and in my opinion, it's just a story.

I believe that real learning takes place in the absence of stories and formulas. Stories can be helpful and inspirational if they help lead you toward your own experience, but if you blindly follow them and deny your experience, you won't really learn. You play golf artistically when you give up your stories and merge with your experience of the game. And one thing I can say for certain is that if you make that leap and enter the game of golf, you will learn.

When *you* disappear—the thoughts, worries, and judgments you have about yourself—Golf as Art shows up. The resulting void is where all the important discoveries—the personal development, satisfaction, joy, and fulfillment—take place.

Golf as Art recognizes the enormity of the potential of the moment. This can also be called creativity, or the Art of the Possible. It is the realization that what could exist greatly exceeds what does exist, and it keeps each moment vibrant, alive, and full of possibility. When a person plays golf in this way—fully absorbed, fully committed, merging with the game—it is a marvelous thing. It is extraordinary golf.

AFTERWORD

Many of the essential concepts of this book—shifting your point of view, increasing awareness, living in the moment, and others—are likely already familiar to you. They are definitely "in the air" and are increasingly becoming part of public discourse, from books to bumper stickers—to golf.

Maybe it's just wishful thinking, but it's not hard to believe that something special is happening. There is a sense—a hope—of the emergence of a new way of looking at the world. The first step in such a change is intellectual understanding, but this needs to be followed by experience—doing. For example, if I'm trying to live fully in the present moment, it doesn't quite work for me to just stand here and say, "Okay, here I am!" I feel it's necessary to have an activity, a vehicle for transformation. There are any number of wonderful activities that can be used in this way, from meditation to running to martial arts to needlepoint. Almost anything will work. My practice is golf, and I think it's a great one.

To be truly effective, a practice must work on all levels:

from a simple, enjoyable activity to a profound and mystical experience. I think golf does this beautifully. A practice also needs to be something that is easy to keep in perspective, something you do not get caught up in and do only for its own sake. This is where golf particularly excels. The game is so darn funny! Sure, it's possible to take golf too seriously, but I don't see how people can do it for too long. I mean, spending thousands of dollars and thousands of hours to learn the best way to hit a little ball into a little hole! Are you kidding? But of course, it's also profound and magical, and we love it. It's perfect.

The next time you play golf, stop for a moment to look closely at a blade of grass. This tiny object is a living thing. It takes in sunlight, water, and air and makes food from them in a way that we know but don't really understand. It's quite a miracle. But it's also just plain grass and it's everywhere and it can be a pain in the neck to take care of. It has the potential to be all those things all the time. And golf is the same way.

The possibilities for golf to be extraordinary are always there, like the grass under your feet. Becoming aware of these possibilities is an art that I have tried to describe here. Golf has many levels, from the simple to the profound, and you can play the game on any of them. I urge you to explore the richness of the game and enjoy this freedom. But I also urge you to relax and take your time. The deeper levels of the game have always been there and always will be there, so you don't have to hurry.

But if you're ready, why wait?

EXERCISES

$\mathbf{T}$he main theme of this book is that extraordinary changes come from a new point of view. Traditional golf teaching focuses almost solely on actions and tends not to look for the deeper causes of those actions. Traditional golf says, "If you learn how to play better, you will be a better golfer." Extraordinary golf says, "If you change the type of golfer that you are, you will play better." Both have the same goals—increased enjoyment, performance, and satisfaction when you play—but they approach them quite differently.

You can read these exercises from either perspective. You can scan them for tips, in the traditional way of looking for quick fixes to apply immediately to your swing. If you do, the results will probably be what they usually are with this method: mild improvement that doesn't last long, then on to the next golf book.

Or, instead of narrow and short-term, you can think broad and long-term. Consider the possibility of a path that leads toward mastery of the game, a path that includes not only how you play but also the type of person you can become. Consider questions that can apply not only to golf but to all areas of your life, such as "What are my commitments?" "How can I learn to trust myself?" "How can I learn how to learn?" Consider the possibility that you can become more and more able to coach yourself and keep yourself on this path.

The main barrier between you and mastery of the game is self-interference. The self that interferes is the you that you think you should be, the identity that you need to let go of before you can leap into the game. Self-interference is what clogs the void—the space that opens when you let go of your stories—where learning takes place. Either you have self-interference or you have nothing, and this nothingness allows for the development of awareness that results in learning. Recognizing self-interference is the first step in getting past it, and the key to recognizing self-interference is the ability to change your point of view.

FIRST EXERCISE: PUTTING

Go out to the putting green and line up a fifteen- or twenty-foot putt, but don't use a ball—just imagine that a ball is there. Look down to where the ball should be, close your eyes, and turn your putter upside down. Keeping your eyes closed, walk toward the hole and try to put the shaft of your putter in the hole. Don't count your steps. Do this same thing three or four times from different distances.

In doing this exercise with many groups of people, I've found that about 80 percent of them stop short of the hole. Very few people ever walk past the hole. Why is this? When most people line up a putt, they usually only look at the area between the golf ball and the hole, which is the end of their known area—the end of their world, so to speak. People are naturally hesitant to enter unknown areas, and this is why in this exercise they tend to approach the hole cautiously, and usually stop short of it.

This is a limited point of view, and the actions in this exercise and in actual putting illustrate it. Your putting stroke reflects the way you see the world. It is very difficult to get people to free up their putting stroke—to let it go, to let it be bold and confident—when the hole is at the edge of their known world. So instead of trying to just change these actions, let's first alter the point of view.

I'd like you to repeat the exercise, but this time when you line up the putt, don't just look at the hole but look also at what's behind it—the edge of the green, the trees, the hillside. See the hole as the middle of something, rather than the edge of something. See it anchored in space, see it in relation to everything around it. Most people lose this sense of perspective and are blind to the surroundings. See the whole picture.

Take the walk again from different distances. Is there more freedom to it? Do you trust your walk more? Can you approach the hole without being afraid? As you become clearer about the spatial relationships and walk more confidently, your putting stroke will change. I have discovered in this exercise that great putters always walk close to the hole without a lot of fear.

In this exercise and the ones that follow, the goal is to change your point of view, and by doing so to get more in touch with your instincts and learn to trust them. The exercises should leave you trusting yourself more and enable you to be your own coach. The exercises here are only a few of the many that my colleagues and I use. They will give you a good sense of the fundamentals of extraordinary golf.

CHAPTER ONE: THE COURSE WALK

We usually describe a round of golf focusing only on the shots we hit and ignoring the time between them. But suppose we were to shift the focus of golf so that the time between shots became everything and the shots themselves meant nothing. This exercise is about making full use of the time between shots.

First, pick a goal for your next round of golf and write down a commitment that you make based on that goal. This could be a commitment to be aware of and present to your actual experience, rather than your belief about your experience. Most people have an ongoing story complete with reasons and judgments about their round of golf that they update with each shot. For example, you hit your ball in the trees. What story do you make up? "I'm playing lousy." "I pulled off the ball." "This is a difficult hole." What is true is that the ball went twenty yards off line into the trees. Period. Everything else is just a story. In this example, you would try to distinguish what actually happens from the story that you make up, the story that keeps you living "in your head" and reduces your awareness, your creativity, and your ability to create a future free from your past.

Other possible commitments are playing without fear, being more open to others, not becoming upset over poor shots, etc.—whatever is important to you. You'll know the right one because it will make you smile when you write it. The point of this round will be to use the time between shots to notice what gets between you and your commitment.

CHAPTER TWO: PURPOSE

My experience tells me that to achieve joy, satisfaction, and fufillment from golf, you need to clarify what you really want, rather than expecting your real goals just to "happen" while you try for something else. This exercise is simple: Write down what you really want when you play golf.

Give the question some thought because it's easy to want what golf society says you should want—performance and achievement. Make sure you choose things that really make you happy. If this question takes you beyond golf and into other areas of your life, all the better. Finding out and writing down what really makes you happy is a very worthwhile thing, and it can often surprise you.

CHAPTER THREE: THE CULTURE OF GOLFERS

For this exercise, go to the driving range and get a bucket of balls. Hit them for half an hour and don't try to fix anything. See if you can become more aware of your swing, your body, and the target. Notice the thoughts that arise as you do this: "This is right." "This is wrong." "Got to fix this." "Why didn't I do that?" "Got to do more of this." The chatter will be there as usual, but maybe this time you can just let it be and not react to it. This means no swing thoughts, no corrections. If you hit it left, don't try to hit it back to the right. Just hit it again. No evaluations, no judgments. Just be aware of the chatter and bring yourself back to observing your game.

This may take time, but stay with it. You'll be amazed at what can happen when you are simply committed to observing and not caught in the fixing-it Culture of Golfers. If you can last half an hour without going crazy, congratulations! You're on your way.

CHAPTER FOUR: CONCENTRATION

Concentration, as we have defined it, is the ability to stay with reality for about two seconds, the time it takes to swing the golf club. This exercise is about discovering the blind spots in your swing—those areas in which you lose concentration and are no longer aware of what you're actually doing.

There are only four things in golf that have real substance: the ball, the club, your body, and the environment—the target. Pick one of the four things—for example, the golf ball. Find something about the ball that interests you, such as the sparkles of the sunlight, the pattern of shadow, or the lettering. Go ahead and take a swing and see if you are able to maintain focus on that element. For what percentage of the swing were you fully with the golf ball? Swing again, and this time note at what point you lose your focus—the specific parts of your swing where you are unable to pay attention to the golf ball. Maybe it's halfway up on the backswing, maybe at the top, maybe as you start down, maybe at impact. There may be more than one. Sense where these blind spots are. You might even want to take a pad and draw a stick figure of a golfer with a club to record the blind spots of each swing. Continue this exercise with the golf ball for about ten minutes.

Then, switch your focus to the head of the club. Track the head of the club throughout all 540 degrees of arc—all the way back and all the way around. Note the blind spots and write them down. Now compare the blind spots when you track the club head to the blind spots when you are looking at the golf ball—are they the same?

Continue this exercise, this time focusing on a part of your body, like the left foot or right shoulder. See if you can stay with the focus throughout the two seconds of your swing. Use stick figures to keep track, and compare them to the others. Notice which of the foci had the fewest blind spots. Anyone who can consistently be present to either the golf ball, the club, a part of the body, or the target will be a very fine golfer.

CHAPTER FIVE: INSTINCTIVE KNOWLEDGE

This is the club-throwing exercise, so let me give you some words of caution. A thrown club can be a dangerous object. It is possible in these exercises to throw the club a lot farther and a lot more off line than you expect. The area all around you should be clear, even in back (I have seen clubs go backward), and when you are doing the full swing you should have at least fifty yards of space in front of you. Pay particular attention to the "hook" direction (left for a right-handed golfer, right for a left-handed one) because clubs are very likely to go that way, and travel a fair distance. Please be careful, and use old clubs.

The purpose of these exercises is to establish a connection between the ball, the club, your body, and the target. In the concentration exercises, the aim was to maintain focus on a single, real thing throughout the two seconds of the swing. The golf ball, the club, and the body were used as objects of focus. But since the target is the ultimate objective in golf, the question arises: How can I focus all my attention on something like the golf ball and still be aware of the target? From studying concentration for the last twenty years, I have found that it is not exclusive: You can include both the ball and the target in your focus. This is clear from the way you drive a car. Your immediate attention is on the traffic and the road conditions, but you are also aware of where you are going. Your destination—your target—guides you. It's your goal, and you never lose awareness of it. Knowing where you're going is the key, as these exercises will show.

The first part concerns chipping. Find an open grassy area that's at least fifty feet long. Grab an iron—it doesn't matter which one—and take a chipping stance, with your target a spot about twenty-five feet ahead. With your eyes on the target, take a normal chipping stroke and release the club toward the target. Repeat with the other irons. Get a feeling for the action of tossing and how it relates to the target: how far the hands go back, the hand position when the club head passes through the middle point, how the body moves. Toss about twenty or thirty clubs.

Next, do the same thing, but close your eyes when the club starts back. Toss the club toward the target you have in your mind's eye. Again, toss twenty or thirty clubs this way, just getting the feel of it. Remember, no evaluations, no judgments, only awareness. Then, take your normal chipping club, keep your eyes on the target, and take the same tossing swing, but this time don't let the club go. Keep taking swings and see if you can feel what happens.

As in all the exercises, understanding what's going on is the lowest rung on the ladder of development. It's not what you understand but what you experience that's the important thing.

Now chip some balls about the same distance you were tossing the club. See if you experience any difference between the throwing motion and the chipping motion. That's the whole game—feeling differences. Experiencing what's possible (club-throwing swing) and experiencing what you do (regular swing) make you aware of the gap between them. In sensing these differences, you'll actually feel the position that's necessary to produce excellent chipping. Learning in golf is the ability to sense the differences between the two motions.

In the second part of this exercise, repeat the four activities—1) throw clubs looking at the target; 2) throw clubs with eyes closed; 3) look at the target and take the throwing motion, but hold onto the club; 4) chip some balls about the same distance as the throw—but this time change the focus. Focus now on distinguishing your natural timing—that of the club-throwing swing—from the timing when you actually hit the golf ball. Are they the same or not?

Pay attention to the club rising, the movements of the body, and the time the swing takes. How long does it take for the body to move back and forth? Where is the acceleration and how soon after you start the downswing does it begin? How does this change in the different swings? The moment you try to fix your swing you'll be unable to sense the timing, and the exercise won't have much value. Be patient and stay with the awareness, and you will begin to discover the timing that you naturally have.

The first part of this exercise was to notice the technique of how things happen. The second part was to notice the timing of how things happen. Now this third part is to notice the balance. Repeat the sequence, but this time take a new focus. How is the body centered when you throw a club? Where does your weight move? Where do you feel on balance and where off balance? Feel for any difference between the balance when you throw a club and the balance when you chip a ball.

When you begin to make some distinctions from these exercises, you're ready to go further. Take it into pitching. Do the same steps as above, but this time hit thirty- to fifty-yard shots. (Remember the warnings I mentioned at the beginning of the chapter, and make sure there is enough room.) You won't be able to throw the clubs as far as you hit the shots, but that doesn't matter—just toss the clubs as far toward the target as the pitching swing will allow. Become aware of the technique, the timing, and the balance. When you begin to develop distinctions here, then you're ready take it to the full swing. But don't rush yourself. Don't think quick fix, think mastery. A good principle to go by is to swing the club only as fast as you can feel it without major blind spots. In the pitching swing and the full swing you may not be able to toss the clubs straight at first—you will likely hold on too long and throw toward your "hook" direction. But keep your focus on the target and soon the clubs will go reasonably straight.

This exercise also works for putting (though of course you shouldn't toss clubs on the green, only on the grassy areas nearby). As I said earlier in the book, the timing and the blind spots are similar for all swings.

The main purpose of this whole exercise is to become aware of the relationship between the ball, the club, your body, and the target. Golf is never about just one part, it is about the relationship of all the parts. The cornerstone of this relationship is the target; that will dictate how much body and club are used. From many years of coaching I've noticed that the most important part of the relationship—target awareness—is the one that's most often missing. Changing the point of view from the ball as goal to the target as goal is the key to this exercise.

CHAPTER SEVEN: FEAR, COURAGE, AND TRUST

The exercises I have been describing are in a planned order. The concentration exercise allows you to become more aware of your swing in a nonjudgmental way, which helps you begin to sense your instincts. The club-throwing exercise allows you to experience those instincts and also the relationship of all the parts of your swing—your natural timing. This instinctive swing is one that you can trust, so this exercise is about trusting that swing, and letting go.

Once you really know something you don't have to think about it anymore. You are not thinking now, "I'm reading this book." You know that. You are not thinking, "I'm sitting down." You know that, too. Once you know things, you can release them from your attention. It's the same with your swing. Once you know and trust your swing, you don't have to put your energy into thinking about it and fixing it. All that energy can go into just swinging and letting it go, which is a form of self-expression. Instead of trying to find the right swing (and who you are), you know the right swing (who you are), and you can express yourself.

When you step up to a golf ball, then, there's nothing to remember. You simply acknowledge the target, and let it go. It's the letting go that's the tricky part—that's where the learning will take place. Letting go doesn't mean randomly slashing at the ball. It's a letting go that is appropriate to a target. The target supplies the structure and boundaries within which is freedom; without some boundaries, there can be no real freedom. Once you know your target—where you're going—you can really let it go.

Go to the driving range and tee up ten or more golf balls side by side with about a club head's distance between each. Step up to the first ball, acknowledge the target, and hit the ball. Don't think or analyze, just swing and let it go. Continue down the line without pausing. As you take each swing, rate yourself on a 1-to-10 scale: ten being complete letting go, one being controlled, manipulative, contrived, or stiff. The point is not to rate the shots themselves but simply the degree of freedom. However, I think you'll be surprised at the shots you hit. You might want to start this exercise small, with chipping, and then progress as in the previous exercise. You may find that your body has been held in check for so long that it's quite difficult to let go. Questions and even fears will arise: Is it okay? What will happen? Will I look bad? The only way to find the answers is to just do it.

The second part of this exercise concerns overcoming these fears. Become aware of the body sensations and thought patterns that you label as fear. See them without interpretation, simply as things that happen. A thought happens and a sensation happens. Fear is only in the interpretation. Notice how these thoughts and sensations, when interpreted as fear, can stop you. When you are hitting it off line, notice the sensations and thoughts that say,

"Something is wrong here; I can't get it." Even when you are hitting it really well, you'll think, "Can I keep it up?" You will begin to see how much fear is present during your practice and your play.

The opposite of fear is letting go. The opposite of fear is trust. Only when you become aware of the sensations and the conversations you have inside your head can you let them go. You don't have to believe them; you don't have to buy into what they say. The point of this whole exercise is very simple—just let it go. One of the main premises of our workshops is that when the joy of letting go becomes more important to you than the quality of your shots, the quality of your shots will amaze you, and you will have truly become a golfer.

Because we've all had the sense that something is possible for us beyond our ordinary game.

THE
SCHOOL FOR EXTRAORDINARY GOLF

Committed to shifting the culture of golf from one of tips, techniques, and formulas to one of exploration, discovery, and freedom.

The School for Extraordinary Golf

P.O. Box 22731
Carmel, CA 93922
1-800-541-2444
Fax: 1-408-625-1976

Three locations in California:

- Carmel-Monterey
- Napa Valley
- Palm Springs

ABOUT THE AUTHORS

Fred Shoemaker's School for Extraordinary Golf is based in Carmel Valley, California. He also teaches the Golf in the Kingdom seminar at the Esalen Institute and is a featured instructor at PGA-sponsored clinics for professionals. Shoemaker, who has given instructional seminars across the United States, in Canada, and in Japan, lives in Carmel Valley.

Pete Shoemaker is a professional software designer, singer, and songwriter whose current recording is the companion to this book, *Extraordinary Golf: Songs of a Wonderful Game*, recently released by BMG Records. A golfer since the age of twelve, he lives in Pacifica, California.

The long-awaited companion volume to
Extraordinary Golf

~ ~ ~

EXTRAORDINARY PUTTING
Endless Fascination

FRED SHOEMAKER
with Jo Hardy

~ ~ ~

On sale January 2006

G.P. Putnam's Sons